# SOUL
# GARDENING

*Cultivating*
*the Good Life*

D0969455

TERRY HERSHEY

**Augsburg**
MINNEAPOLIS

*For Judith and Zachary*

SOUL GARDENING
Cultivating the Good Life

Cover design by Michelle L. Norstad and David Meyer
Cover image from Tony Stone Images. Used by permission.
Book design by Michelle L. Norstad

Scripture passages marked NEB are from *The New English Bible,* copyright © 1961, 1970 by the Delegates of the Oxford University Press and the Syndics of the Cambridge University Press. Reprinted by permission.

Scripture passages marked RSV are from the *Revised Standard Version* of the Bible, copyright © 1946, 1952, 1971, 1989 by the Division of Christian Education of the National Council of the Churches of Christ in the USA. Used by permission.

*Library of Congress Cataloging-in-Publication Data*
Hershey, Terry, 1954–
  Soul gardening : cultivating the good life / Terry Hershey.
    p. cm.
  Includes bibliographical references.
  ISBN 0-8066-4037-5 (alk. paper)
    1. Spiritual life. 2. Gardening—Religious aspects. 3. Hershey, Terry, 1954– I. Title.
BL624.H45 2000
291.4'4—dc21
                                              99-53603

Manufactured in the U.S.A.

AF 9-4037

# TABLE
OF CONTENTS

# ACKNOWLEDGMENTS

The *Soul Gardening* journey began when I planted a flower and lost track of time while meandering about the garden. Just for the sake of meandering. Two things I discovered: One, meandering is good for whatever ails you. Two, there are wonderful people to meet along the garden path. People who taught me, encouraged me, and supported me. And I am grateful to them all.

If you are a writer, you can do no better than to join a writer's group—like-minded folk who meet regularly to read one another's work in order to make it better. Four years ago, I happened on such a group. I had already been putting my musings on paper, and this group listened to every word and, in the end, made *Soul Gardening* a better book.

Thank you to the fine group of writers who critiqued and supported: Betty Sorrels, Linda Malnack, Sam Sutherland, Nancy Sorenson, Gerry Sorenson, Mary O'Malley, and Sarah-Jane Menato. And to our group's leader, Ellie Bator, who edited my preliminary work, and continued to push and cheer, a special thank you.

Early on, Jessica Maxwell helped with insight and direction from her own journey as author, lover of nature, and spiritual pilgrim. And other friends pitched in with words of affirmation and counsel. Thanks to Tom Thompson, Alan Loy McGinnis, and Mary Alice Kier.

The publication of this book with Augsburg Fortress was born out of a friendship with Ron Klug and the weekly tidbits about the good life that we exchanged—notes about those few things that really matter: roaming the garden, living with good music, enjoying good food, embracing family and friends. Our paths crossed because another mutual friend, Harold Ivan Smith, knew that both Ron and I loved the garden, and Harold knew, intuitively, that gardeners relish the company of other gardeners.

So a special thank you to my editor and soul gardening friend, Ron Klug, who knows the value of an afternoon spent hiking the back forty and gets goose bumps at the sight of a wild turkey with her chicks.

And thanks to Martha Rosenquist and Tim Larson, and all those at Augsburg Fortress whose dedicated work guided this book through the maze of proofreading, publication, printing, and publicizing. I am indebted.

When I go home, my wife and I—dragged by our two-year-old son—like to wander the garden, just to see what has gone on in our absence. "Let's go check out the garden," we tell Zachary, and off we go. On this day, the sun has already sunk beyond the tree line, and the plants are enhanced, now a darker shade. The volume of the day's clamor, as if linked to the sun's setting, is turned down. I hear my son laugh, see him race around the grass paths, and it hits me—I'm lucky and blessed all in one and, quite frankly, it doesn't get any better than this.

*Deep within us all there is an amazing inner sanctuary of the soul,*
*a holy place, a Divine Center, a speaking Voice, to which we may*
*continuously return. Eternity is at our hearts, pressing upon our*
*time-torn lives, warming us with intimations of an astounding*
*destiny, calling us home unto Itself. Yielding to these persuasions,*
*gladly committing ourselves in body and soul, utterly and*
*completely, to the Light Within, is the beginning of true life.*
*It is a dynamic center, a creative Life that presses to birth*
*within us. It is a Light Within which illumines the face of God*
*and casts new shadows and new glories upon the face of men.*
*It is a seed stirring to life if we do not choke it.*
— Thomas Kelly

# INTRODUCTION

*A Zen roshi is dying. All of the monks gather—*
*an eagerness restrained—around the deathbed,*
*hoping to be chosen as the next teacher.*
*The roshi asks slowly, "Where is the gardener?"*
*"The gardener," the monks wonder aloud. "He is just a simple man*
*who tends the plants, and he is not even ordained."*
*"Yes," the roshi replies. "But he is the only one awake.*
*He will be the next teacher."*
—Zen Story

There is a wondrous and incurable obsession, which takes you meandering to garden paths. Just for the sake of meandering. Of course, the obsessed tend toward jealous excess. I will be unable to hide my proclivity for the sacred necessity of Adirondack chairs, my infatuation with old garden roses, my enchantment with early summer's butterfly cabaret, or my distrust of anyone who is put off by dirty fingernails. Just so you are forewarned.

I recently had lunch with a friend who was visiting the Seattle area from Florida's west coast. He is in his late thirties, an achiever, and a success in his business endeavors. Eighteen months ago, he became a homeowner for the first time and now is enthralled with the small yard he has, stuffed to the gills with a hodgepodge of herbage: coffee plants from Guatemala, dwarf citrus trees, a passion fruit vine, varieties of hot peppers, and a mélange of vegetables. All of this is in the middle of a city, in a lot no larger than a racquetball court. He gushed, like any unsullied convert, and worried, knowing that Florida's weather reached below freezing and into the twenties through the night. It was all he could do to not cut his business trip short in order to rush home and check on the well-being of his baby pepper plants.

The garden captures us. We fall prey to an inoperable madness.

I have another friend who admits, with some mild chagrin, "When I get home from work, I rush out into the garden to see what has bloomed in my absence, all before I think about feeding my kids." Her husband looks on, rolling his eyes.

My friend's stories make me smile and laugh and relive my own fall from sanity. We come to recognize that conspicuous glow and sense of wonder that characterizes kindred spirits on the garden path. If we are lucky, we are the unwitting recipients of a spell far greater than we had hoped for or foreseen. For gardening allows us to make a holy place to serve the soul. Which makes this a spiritual endeavor, and difficult to talk about in this culture because it smacks of some truth reduced to a bumper sticker. But spirituality is another way of saying that life and reality are more than a sum of their parts and more than the answers we deduce from those sums—a good reminder especially for me, whose world reeked of implied spirituality.

The word *spirituality* has been suspect for some time, conjuring images of the fervid and the unctuous, people who could benefit from a substantial amount of roughage in their diets. Those with apparently no real life to live, spending their energies cashing in their coupons for harps on clouds, streets of gold up yonder, and all that.

This spirituality, however, is not about a lottery ticket to the next life, but a front-row-center ticket to this one. This life, with its car pools, ill-timed meetings, bleating pagers, demanding children, traffic snarls, and yammering pain-in-the-neck obligations. This life, where once in a while, just for a minute, you stop what you are doing and watch the clouds roll through the northern sky, a conveyor belt of fleece. The wind is out of the southwest, filling your lungs, and you catch a glimpse of a blue heron, gliding like a javelin across the sky. This world now on center stage, no longer peripheral to your duties and obligations. And the full weight of this moment seeps its way back into the grind of the everyday, slowing our heartbeat, giving us a gentler step and a gleam in the eye.

Late in her life, May Sarton was questioned about what she wanted to be when she "grew up." She replied, "To be human."

Not bad.

To be human is about regaining what has been lost in the shuffle when life has been relegated to keeping score and making waves. To be human is about cultivating the good life. To be human is about gardening the soul.

You can count me in if it means cultivating a place where I am attentive, present, and grounded. It's just that twenty years of relentless pursuit of the good life delivered by a lottery-driven culture had rendered my perspective noticeably one-dimensional—what's the payoff?—as if consumption equals life at its finest.

Now, my questions have begun to change: Are there butterflies in your garden? Are there dandelions in your lawn? And when was the last time your house smelled of paper-white narcissus?

Do sunsets make you smile? Have you ever seen a sunflower bloom? At what angle does the sun enter your house? And when do your irises blossom? Are you comforted by the sound of the rain on your roof? And have you ever watched the hummingbirds dance?

I love to watch the hummingbirds dance.

And I love spring nights here. The days are already longer, the skies backlit until past nine. The backlighting gives the horizon its density. Off to the north sits Blake Island, home to nothing but cedar and hemlock and fir and a couple of eagles. In the dusk light, the island puts on a thickness as if the deep colors anchor it to the earth.

I love that my two-year-old son likes to put on his dancing shoes. The music doesn't matter. He's not picky. He just loves to dance. Like the hummingbirds.

I love to stretch out on a garden bench on a warm summer day.

I love a hot shower and drying with an expensive oversized cotton towel.

I treasure the certainty that grace gives us all many second chances.

And I love to lose track of time in my garden.

I once asked my analyst why I was in therapy. He told me it would make me a better gardener. Gardening can be strong medicine— an elixir that nurtures and shapes the soul. For that reason, it is a tonic seldom taken straight with no ice. Gardening has a way of seeping into your soul, and one day you find yourself, in the words of the poet May Sarton in *Plant Dreaming Deep,* spending the first half hour of the morning "enjoying the air and watching for miracles."

That's the way it happened to me.

Fortuitously, these are not lessons learned from books or classes. You are compelled to meander, if only in the garden of your mind. Better yet, the process demands putting your hands in the soil, letting the sun sedate your disquiet and warm your face, feeling your lungs fill with the honeyed sweetness of winter jasmine, or the rambling rector rose, watching a red-tailed hawk surf the currents, savoring the chamomile scent of crushed cedar leaves, allowing the garden to render its power and magic. In a world where we are enamored with image, it is in the garden we are slowly weaned off our steady diet of the spectacular, and the "real story," in order to revel in the daily, the ineffable, the sacred, the surprising. In other words, the garden is a place where it feels good to be alive.

Robert Capon says, "we live life like ill-taught piano students . . . so inculcated with the flub that gets us in Dutch, we don't hear the music; we only play the right notes."

My pedigree is good. Raised in a religious environment and trained in religious colleges and seminaries, I came well equipped to see the world the "right" way. By the age of twenty-five, I became an ordained Protestant clergyman, the fulfillment of a lifelong calling: that thorny mixture of skill, desire, and parental pressure (which began its germination at the age of four in my case, when I was prompted and paraded as the "preacher boy"—all of it heaped with lavish and addictive accolades). At the time, of course, it did not seem unforeseen. Molded from Calvinist clay, I knew my place in this world. And I knew the path expected of me. Life was as it should be: intact and well contained. I pursued my calling with a vengeance, and there is no doubt that I was a success. The bigger the church, the bigger the crowd. The bigger the crowd, the greater the applause. The greater the applause, the bigger the plaques to hang on my office walls. And the preacher boy grew up, and made good.

There is one caveat. To find success doesn't necessarily mean that you gain health. We go about our merry and hectic way, accumulating and weighing, measuring and posturing, hoping that the balance sheet of life judges us with kindness. Until that one day when you look into the mirror and ask yourself, "Why?" and you decide then and there to set about reclaiming that which has been lost—namely, you.

I do know this. I did not set out to find answers, health, the good life, or even God. In fact, I did not "set out" at all. I knew only that my soul felt malnourished. Then one day I found myself in the garden, and quite without fanfare, the journey began.

Soul gardening is not a cause-and-effect proposal. It happens when you least expect it, germinating when the ground is fertile and primed.

It was scheduled as "boy's weekend out." Five friends hurtling down the Colorado River, a white-water raft our ticket to peril and pleasure. We had been plotting this day, determining ways to make it a sport, a contest, talking big about our fearlessness and our desire for serious rapids. We were, after all, real men, all belly and bravado, and nature's playground beckoned.

The sun reigned high over an expansive Colorado mountain sky, endless and open, bleached of any rich or subtle hues. The sun baked our faces while continual sprays of river water baptized us with exhilaration. We whooped and cavorted and egged each other on. We looked forward to that evening in the Jacuzzi, beer in hand, telling and retelling the day, a forum for exaggeration and blarney about our exploits.

While the rafting crew worked to pull the raft from the water after our run was completed, I climbed the embankment and sat on a rock near the top, drinking in the warmth of afternoon. The area near me was littered with woody mountain shrubs. Something else caught my eye. Over the embankment to my left, growing from a ledge, stood a single clump of iris, sixteen inches high, a desert gemstone in a rich azure luster. I scrambled down near the ledge and gaped, frozen as if in the company of a magical snow leopard. I touched its delicate falls like the face of a lover.

I didn't exactly know who to tell, or what exactly I would say: "Hey guys. Come up here and check out this flower!"

That would have gone over big.

I do know that my hand shook as if I were overcome with awe. A Barbara Kingsolver line came to mind: "A great many people will live out their days without ever seeing such sights, or if they do, never gasping."

I felt lucky. And I knew. This is why I had come to Colorado. A single iris arresting something rudimentary in me. All my previous priorities paled. For neither my résumé nor my clerical collar mattered one whit.

For most of my life, my spirituality had depended upon answers. Sitting on an embankment above the Colorado River, I had none. Only the glow of a flower, the warmth of the sun, and the invigoration of the river's energy and strength. I had only mystery and awe. And peace. For once there was no compulsion to explain, or clarify, or analyze. Which meant that I was lost in the moment—what some Catholics have called the Sacrament of the Present Moment—seeing each "present moment" as diffused with holiness. It reminded me of Susanna Wesley's immortal prayer, "Help me, Lord, to remember that religion is not to be confined to the church, or closet, nor exercised only in prayer and meditation, but that everywhere I am in Thy presence."

So I sat for a spell in that presence, and at home.

Here's the quandary: How do you tell someone that you were unraveled by an iris? It's not exactly fodder for small talk.

Like it or not, the card deck of life's priorities is reshuffled in moments like that. Your résumé takes a back seat, and you scramble up the embankment with a new posture, and a new frame of reference, knowing that your load is a little lighter even though you hold something new and sacred in your heart.

I was raised in the heartland of America, where gardening meant one thing: drudgery. Plain and simple. Drudgery—as in to till and to hoe and to weed. Especially to weed.

I am still a Midwestern boy at heart and take delight in vivid memories of lilacs' spring pungency, mown grass, backyard baseball, straight-edged cornfields, imposing black-trunked oaks, and the crunch of a radish pulled fresh from the soil. And yet, like most of my generation from small Midwestern towns, I couldn't wait to leave.

My journey took me through California, where I spent the formative years of my adult life absorbing the notion that image is everything and that substance can be sacrificed for immediacy. I acquired a taste for the enamor of glitter and hype, furthering my detachment from the land. But not without a price. It slowly consumed pieces of my soul. It is, however, not all for naught. In California began my affair with the rose and my passion for plants. But I was not yet a gardener. Unbeknownst to me, there was a conversion afoot.

Fifteen years and fifteen hundred miles separate me from the boy in that young man. The boy in this gardener is not the same boy anymore. He's not so mercurial about dirty fingernails. He is bewitched by the scent of the Asiatic lily 'Casablanca.' He's an avid student in the art of "sitting in the garden." Some days it is enough to wrestle and loll on the grass paths with Conroy, his ebullient black Lab. His head goes loopy at the sight of forsythia blooms in late winter.

Today, I am a writer. A gardener. And a pilgrim. But not necessarily in that order. And I must confess to you that as pilgrims go, I'm of a most improper sort.

But don't for a minute think that I have given up "preaching the word." It's just that now my pulpit is an old bench under the plum tree where I'm fortified by the bracing scent of a honeysuckle vine. The pews are patches of dandelion-filled-lawn off to the side of the wood fence on which the honeysuckle climbs. A trio of Swainson's thrush forms our choir. It is Sacrament Sunday. But then every day is Sacrament Sunday. The sermon today is "Cultivating the Good Life by Embracing the Art of Doing Nothing."

I have a friend who gives me grief for what he calls my "sell all and flee to the country" sermon. There's no doubt, I do get worked up. And I'll be the first to admit that moving for the sake of moving is not the answer, either. There is certainly no formula here. But I dare you to sit on this bench with me, long enough to let the honeysuckle warm your blood and soothe your spirit and reconnect you with something fundamental and sacred.

Before you know it, the passion takes root. It's only a matter of time.

Whenever I lecture about gardens, I'm introduced as an expert. But I do not consider myself so. This book is a call for amateurs, those of us who enjoy the air and watch for miracles. *Amateur,* that is, from the French: "one who loves" or "for the love of." *Amateur* is that part of us still thrilled by the miraculous sweetness of a freshly picked strawberry, or by the amazing display of new perennial shoots each spring, or by the way the wind drifts through wind chimes, heartfelt as a prayer, or by the reassuring strains of contented chatter coming from the finches who convene at back-deck feeders.

Somewhere along the way, there is something that gets under our skin. And that something begins to slowly transform us from the inside, regardless of whether we've ever planted a garden, or whether we know a Delphinium from a daisy.

Across the continent from my childhood home, I live above a canyon, on an island in Puget Sound, in a cabin where my wife has lived for twelve years.

We sit on the deck and look down through the crease of hemlock and western red cedar. "When I first came here," she tells me, "I was enchanted. And I still am."

I now know why.

# SPRING

---

*To embrace the value of idleness . . .*
*To see ordinary gifts of grace*

# ONE

## SPEND THE AFTERNOON

*Spend the afternoon. You can't take it with you.*
—Annie Dillard

*Speak to your heart in silence upon your bed.*
—Psalm 4:4, RSV

*He lacks much who has no aptitude for idleness.*
—Louise Beebe Wilder

I am just on the edge of sleep, adrift in that kingdom where images move with exaggerated pace—as if the dreamworld carousel surrenders its final pirouettes, and gravity regains its dominion. Bees, nature's incantatory pollen couriers, furnish a hypnotic drone, the perpetual melody of early summer's symphony. The sun is a benevolent comforter, and the smell of fresh-cut grass brings back the baseball games of my youth. My pillow—my accommodating black Labrador, Conroy—rises and falls with each breath. My cap is pulled down over my eyes, and I dream of hitting a game-winning home run. The air is close, suffused with the scent of Conroy's warm skin. We have nowhere to go this day and are in no hurry to get there.

But it has not always been this way. I was bent on being the young clergyman making his mark on this world. Not that we former clergy have a monopoly on this infection. It seems to taint us all. It's just that I was rewarded—ironically—for my hell-bent pace. We church folk were encouraged to burn ourselves out for God—conjuring images of one so weary with well doing he begins to smolder at the collar and eventually spontaneously combusts, to perpetual sainthood. A fate which won great respect and added, I was proud to divulge, plaques to my wall.

Suffice it to say, I never heard or preached any sermons on the necessity of slowing down—let alone the art of doing nothing. I lived unwittingly chained to the cardinal rule that it didn't matter if you didn't know where you were going, it was the ultimate of bad form to be late. For time, of course, is money. And money, of course, is everything, or any of a veritable smorgasbord of medicinal clichés.

On one of my pilgrimages to southwestern England (like a compass pointed north, we fledgling gardening converts seek out great garden meccas), I made some effort to locate the gardens of Mirabel Osler. I have never met Mirabel Osler (and never did find her garden), but I am indebted to her. Her book, *A Gentle Plea for Chaos,* has become one of my sacred texts. Mirabel is, most importantly, a self-described "unserious gardener." This "unseriousness" stands in contrary distinction to those "proper gardeners," or those who "never sit in their gardens." These proper gardeners are, Osler tells us, "dedicated and single-minded" to a fault in that "the garden draws them into its embrace where their passions are never assuaged unless they are on their knees." In sharp contrast are "the unserious, the improper people, who plant and drift, who prune and amble—we fritter away little dollops of time in sitting about our gardens."

Osler is gardening's patron saint for the freedom to loll.

Gardening begins here. Sitting. Lolling. There are no shortcuts. My temptation—as a new gardener—was to dash off to the local nursery, load up on color, inject seedlings into the soil, and expect an immediate payoff. This can hardly be a surprise, as I lived that way in all areas of my life. We can safely infer that "freedom to loll" struck me as an exercise utterly foreign to my busy, religious, performance-oriented world.

In an unpretentious little book on garden benches, Osler makes no bones about her shibboleth: "I am deeply committed to sitting in the garden."

Amen. And Amen.

In 1625, Francis Bacon wrote that gardening is the purest of human pleasures, the greatest refreshment to the spirits of man. No argument here. But ask ten different gardeners just exactly what Bacon had in mind, and you'll get ten different answers. Therein lies the conundrum. That in the process of becoming a gardener— eager for any advice, counsel, suggestions—you are subject to many mixed messages about gardening's very raison d'être. We find ourselves in a quandary predicated on the preposterous Western assumption that everything exists for some function.

This goes way back. To Eden. You see, even before God's warnings about thorns and thistles and wild plants, the implication was that gardening is work. Apparently, we were put in the Garden of Eden to till it and care for it. Okay so far.

I'm the first to recognize the soothing gratification at the end of a gardening day in the sweet aftertaste of muscle ache, sweat, and the visible results of our labor (newly tilled soil, paver neatly joined, an overgrown thicket systematically subdued). These are our flags of achievement. But what of the part about the purest of human pleasure?

Osler plays devil's advocate: "Sitting in your own garden is a feat to be worked at with unflagging determination and single-mindedness—for what gardener worth his salt sits down?"

It is the connection or association of work with refreshment that gives us fits. And the part about how it all should add up to some sense of general well-being. How do we maintain an ethic of hard work and still give ourselves permission to shut down without feeling guilt or remorse? Or worse, how do we ignore the lingering accusation of wasted time? There's the rub. It's a hard habit to shake.

The phone rings, disturbing my reverie. A child of my culture, I jump up and scramble to the house to answer. "What are you doing?" the voice inquires.

"Nothing," I answer, winded.

Pause. I sense an arched eyebrow. "Nothing?"

I rack my brain for an appropriate explanation. "Well, I'm in the garden taking a nap with my dog."

"No." Another pause. "No, I mean what are you doing really?"

Oh well. My explanation is unlikely to win sympathy, let alone accolades. The moral is clear: Like big boys who don't cry, real gardeners don't nap with their dogs.

To be sure, the question "what are you doing?" is merely code for "what are you doing that is of importance?" and not all that far removed from "what are you doing of importance with your life?" However we hear the question, it serves to awaken the "proper gardener" in each of us—that wired self, fidgeting over what tasks will earn some merit points today. It's infectious, this notion of our worth tied to our achievements and work, and the carousel spins 'round and 'round.

I remember one conversation with a seat mate, hurtling through space some 30,000 feet above the heartland. "What do you do?" he asked.

"I'm a writer," I answered with the trepidation that comes whenever your value is under scrutiny.

"Oh really, what do you write?"

"Uh, gardening stuff mostly, some personal growth nonfiction, some fiction."

"No kidding. You famous? Would I know any of your books?"

"Probably not. . . . I mean, I haven't published any yet. At least no fiction. . . . I mean, I've published non-fiction," I rambled.

He stared.

Pause.

Then, "Oh." Nothing else. Just, "Oh."

If I were a doctor, effusing would ensue. A psychiatrist, I'd have a client for the remainder of the conversation. A traveling businessman, I'd garner the curiosity and jealousy afforded those who gallivant through airports. But a writer?

How much worse if I told him I was only a gardener?

It sure was easier in the old days, when I could rely on a head-turning answer: "I am a minister." Granted, it too was met with total silence. But at least you could tell that they were impressed. Sooner or later, they would ask my advice about a personal problem "for a friend." One man merely nodded his head and said, apropos of nothing in particular, "That's great. I had an uncle who was a Methodist."

At any rate, I spent the next few days laboring at the computer, purging myself of the guilt I feel misleading another stranger about my relative importance. Writer indeed. There's the catch. Writer, in Americanese, implies "sells books." (I remember reading Philip Roth saying that works of art are utterly useless and terribly important.)

In the meantime, I have been corresponding with a friend for six years. Monthly or bimonthly letters, about life as we see it. Or life as we wish it. Life as we'd make it if we were in charge. These are dispatches of the soul, a weird mixture of story telling, pontificating, postulating, confessing, debating, and male hormonal strutting. One part adolescents playing "king of the mountain." One part amateur ornithologists comparing their lists at the end of a memorable day. You'd think it would be enough for my self-esteem quotient.

There are those lucky days, when the sun illuminates the translucent "bat wing" ruby thorns of the rose *sericea pteracantha,* or a swallow-tail butterfly provides a cabaret while sipping at a wallflower, or a rainbow arches its back through the northern sky after a morning of fateful clouds have skittered and leapt, or daffodils glow, faithful and sanguine around the maple tree, or the summer sun stays in the sky well into evening, letting you sit on the back deck listening to crickets well past bedtime, or the candied scent of a bearded iris transports you back to a high school dance when the best-looking girl in town really did want to drape her arms around your neck during all the slow numbers. Yes, there are those lucky days when public opinion means something only to pollsters and politicians, when you realize that the elastic jurisdiction of what "they" think cannot find you here in this little corner of the globe, and you raise your head to the stars and shout to no one in particular, "If this isn't nice, what is?"

There's a wonderful conversation in *Regarding Henry* (a movie about a conscience-less lawyer who suffers brain damage from a gunshot wound and finds himself recovering in a new and strange world) during which Henry tells his physical therapist, "I tried to go back to my life. But I don't like who I was. I don't fit in." His therapist tells him, "Don't listen to nobody trying to tell you who you are. It may take awhile, but you'll figure yourself out."

Like the young poet who wants Rilke to confirm in him that he is, in fact, a poet, this is all about what tags we hang on our identity. Or whether we compliantly accept what someone else has hung there on our behalf. And how much time we spend fighting ghosts and false expectations.

My preacher boy tag assured me that I knew the formula, and theoretically, knew the formula maker. Even so, I kept my nose clean and prayed for recompense. I continually measured my worth against the formula, and came up wanting. Everything—relationships, vocations, encounters with nature—was measured through this lens of the formula, equal parts effort, zeal, and the accumulation of good deeds. Life, reduced to its parts. Bottom line? My spirituality depended upon answers and performing a role.

So I spent my early years perfecting that role. As one man put it, "You find out what your strengths are, then you get into that persona; you perfect it and costume it and perform it. It comes to feel like you. But the frustration is the feeling: 'That's not the me that I like, or the me that I would like other people to know.' The effort expended in creating and defending that persona is exhausting. Once we stop being ruled by the need to prove ourselves to the world and begin to relax our vigilance around maintaining the false self—what a relief—we can start stripping back down to what is real, not false or copied, to uncover our own authenticity."

And our soul.

Of course, it is not easy, this transition from external to internal affirmation—especially when you have been inculcated in a vocation enamored with surface kudos. My ministerial mask served me well in this capacity, hiding as I did behind a glittering image. Yet the problem isn't solved by changing rank or title. We are more than our labels, which is comforting only on our good days. As much as we hate being pigeonholed or misunderstood, the older we get, the more we hope for some demarcation that provides clarity, that strange attraction to quintessence on our gravestone.

We are drawn to the consummation inherent in this cultural dog-sniffing, "So, what do you do?" I propose that we answer the question honestly. "I read books; I walk my dogs; I work in the garden; I play baseball. . . ." A reply surely to be met with suspicion, more than likely promoting another raised eyebrow.

If you really want an answer to your question, you'll have to spend a day in my garden planting and drifting, fussing and puttering. Yesterday, a package arrived from a nursery. My morning was spent coddling those newborns, settling them in one-gallon containers, allowing them a long cool drink of water while letting them daydream about the back border where they will eventually find a home.

Four hundred years ago, a theologian-mathematician-philosopher named Pascal wrote, "By means of a diversion, a man can avoid his own company twenty-four hours a day."

So we're back to that. You know, the need to sit still. Or in the words of the psalmist, the need to "speak to your heart in silence upon your bed." Which is not so easy to do with this insidious canker to be somebody. Although that's not quite it either. Lily Tomlin once said, "I always wanted to be somebody. I just should have been more specific." So it's not just the being somebody that's at stake here. It's the *being*—or sitting still—with *this* somebody, the freedom to loll and all that with *this* somebody.

"But you still have to work, don't you?"

Indeed. Every morning I write. My office is a loft on the second story of our home. Each afternoon is devoted to garden designs here on the island.

Some days I sit at my computer and just stare out the window. I've read that this is dangerous for a writer, to be distracted in this way. It's best to stare at a plain, grey wall. Let all your energy and focus go into your writing. And not your daydreaming. Good idea. One problem: I live on the top of a knoll on an island in Puget Sound, and my study looks north, down through a canyon of western red cedar, Douglas fir, western hemlock, big-leaf maple, and Pacific madrone onto the slate blue brine. Chekhov talked about the desire to illuminate the actual world with a delicate light. And before you know it, you're caught up, mesmerized by how that actual world enchants and incites. So I stare out my window. Every once in a while I see a bald eagle. There's a pair that nests on the north end of our island. Like seeing someone famous, you halt what you're doing and gawk. There's magisterial ease riding that eight-foot wingspan. You get giddy during these times, and it doesn't matter what follows. The day has been worth living.

Writing begins with the senses, some say. It helps us smell the universe. They got that right. For if you step out onto the deck of our house on a fall morning when the grey canopy of winter solstice has begun to tighten its grip, you can smell the thick wet earth and the candied fragrance of the rambling rose, 'Darlow's Enigma.' And before long, you're hunkered down on a deck chair, cup of Earl Grey in hand, building garden dreams from pictures in your head, gladdened and entertained by the unexpected visit of a regal pileated woodpecker foraging and dancing on an old cedar snag.

There comes an age when the question of what you're going to be when you grow up starts to become moot, and you find yourself needing to paint or get off the ladder with regard to this relentless pressure to arrive somewhere. This is not to say it isn't important to take aim or set goals, or that life doesn't change and grow; it's just that there is no need to assume that life will suddenly kick in when we get to where we're going at such a manic pace. We seem to think that if we try hard enough, we'll get it right this time, all the while fueled by some smoldering resentment for life as it is. We may not like the movie of our life, but that's no reason to ream the projectionist. And it's even crazier if we choose to leave the theater and spend the rest of our days on the defensive.

I try to explain to people that I have made a dramatic change in my life. Emphasis upon *my*. I had no intention of creating a paradigm or a new seminar on life reconstruction. Truth is, one day, quite by happenstance, I planted a flower.

As the flower grew, I began to feel something come alive in my own skin. I would go out at weird hours of the day and night, just to fuss over the flower. I dug in the dirt to the let the flower breathe. I planted other flowers to give the flower friends. And I surprised myself by crying when one of the flowers died for no apparent reason.

I caught myself humming odd melodies from my childhood, blushing, wondering if anyone heard me. As the flowers continued to grow, I took a chair out and sat in the garden just to keep them company. I would tell the flowers funny stories and laugh out loud into the evening sky. A strange grin spread across my face as I realized what was happening. I felt at home.

The months went on. I planted more flowers. I planted vegetables and trees. I brought guests to my garden just to see them smile.

I watched my garden grow. I fussed and frittered. I dug and danced. I came face to face with a part of myself that had been missing. And I liked what I saw.

The garden put me in a frame of mind where I could hear and see and feel again, as if some part of me that had ossified came back to life. I cannot say with certainty that I heard God's voice (for I'm not sure what that voice would sound like were I to hear it), but I suspect that God was the one who planted the seed to begin with, and was watching over me while that seed took root. For in the garden I found, in the words of Quaker teacher Thomas Kelly in *A Testament of Devotion,* the "amazing inner sanctuary of the soul, a holy place, a Divine Center, a speaking Voice."

Sitting in the garden, the Shasta Daisy could care less about my pedigree, which in turn serves as the perfect metaphor for God's grace—an altogether difficult lesson to swallow in a world where all of our encounters seem like contests, where only the winner is granted the right to move on.

There is a time, perhaps early morning, when the air is still full of hope, and the dew crystallizes on the ephemeral petals of the exquisite Japanese iris, 'Kumchi Gumii.' Or maybe the time is dusk on the back deck, cheered by the finches as they vie for seed and hypnotized by the spikelets of rattlesnake grass oscillating in the breeze—when, for reasons not yet fully realized, you start to take back what has been disowned. And maybe, just maybe, you start to slowly embrace what is there, rather than to pine away for tomorrow.

Of course, the theory disintegrates like cheap, wet confetti as soon as you try to analyze it, and make it a system for others to follow. What are those steps again?

There is no doubt that we are a people wired to achieve. Wired to see accomplishment as a sign of our esteem, our worth. It is in our blood, as most of us are unable to make it through the day without our lists, or our Day-Timers. Don't some of us find unmitigated physical ecstasy in crossing off each consummated item? There is palpable relief in this act of cleansing. (Some of us even go so far as to add an item to our list that we've already accomplished, just so that we can cross it off.) Relief in the finality of that unequivocal and orgasmic check mark. Our blood froths with delirium. Which gives us liberty to add two more items to our list.

It seems to me that there is something lost if it becomes necessary to justify a lazy afternoon under the category of time well spent. "Spend the afternoon" is now another contest, rated as if by judges at a diving meet, their placards held high: "8" for "ambling," but only a "5" for "frittering." Which makes us want to sign up for the next class on "Garden Frittering 101."

(It is clear to me now why the whole idea of a "devotional life" [time spent alone in prayer or Bible meditation] was such a thorn in my youth. Apparently, being in the presence of God was not enough, and not nearly as important as studying for some pop quiz. And heaven knows, you didn't want to be found lacking.)

In an enlightened treatise entitled *Waiting for the Weekend,* Witold Rybczynski writes that there is a difference between having *free time* and having *freedom.* In other words, it is plausible to be enslaved by our weekends—it's the proper gardener syndrome all over again—compelled to have a good time. It's like the mother I overheard at Disney World speaking tersely to her three children, "Smile! We're here to have fun. So you'd better start now!" Or the equally compelling story of a woman overheard speaking to her teenage son, who sat morosely in the back of their car, parked at the lookout for Oregon's Mount St. Helens: "Yes, you *will* get out of the car, and you *will* look at the damn mountain. We drove two thousand miles to get here!"

There's a garden contest here in the Seattle area (held in conjunction with our annual Flower and Garden Show), and it has become quite a big deal. Five years ago, before I began my garden design business, I entered and expected to win.

I didn't. And wondered about all the fuss when I saw the pictures of those who did. Three judges (giving you one month's advance notice) visited your garden, clipboards in hand. For that month I worked nonstop, looking at my garden through the eyes of a critic. Of course, the fact that the garden is judged in late July or early August doesn't help. The hardy geraniums are spent and leggy. Empty spaces glare and rebuke where there had bloomed inky delphinium and scarlet poppy. The self-seeded fireweed at the back of the border surely may be considered cluttered, the sign of a gardener remiss. All these gymnastics for a prize. What came over me? And yet, in the evenings, I couldn't help walking through the garden scheming, analyzing, what it would take to win the next year.

There is a story about an obsessive-compulsive American who decided to take an African safari. He plotted the course and determined a timetable, the trip now representing a test or a time trial. He hired coolies from a local African tribe to carry the variety of cases and containers. On the first morning, the entire party roused early, traveled very, very fast and went very, very far. On the second day, they roused early, traveled very, very fast and went very, very far. On the third day, the same. On the fourth morning, the jungle tribesmen refused to move. The American gestured irately and fumed at the translator to get them going. "They will not move," the translator relayed.

"Why not?" the American bellowed, thinking of dollars wasted and time spent.

"Because," the translator told him, "they are waiting for their souls to catch up with their bodies."

It is no secret that our culture is not very good at this—the waiting for the soul part. Some call it idleness. Some call it rest. Some just call it laziness. But others call it play.

The Bible calls it Sabbath. Or, in the words of Thomas Kelly in *Reality and the Spiritual World,* "Listening to the eternal involves a silence within us."

Regardless of the label, the effect is the same. It lets us stop long enough to connect, or reconnect as the case may be, with that "inner sanctuary of the soul . . . a Divine Center, a speaking Voice," to something human and fundamental to being alive.

Outside my window, a male rufous hummingbird—with his zee-chirppity-chirp and glow-in-the-dark carmine-sequined gorget—sits on an outer twig of a neighboring hemlock branch. His head never stops swiveling, and he looks curiously as if he is a caffeine addict or a spectator at a world-championship Ping-Pong tournament. Rufous hummingbirds are adamantly protective of their primary food source. The first bird to discover a source defends it. Finders keepers, losers weepers—a game like king-of-the-mountain where only one can be king. We have three feeders around our house. Each has been claimed by a hummingbird who, though satiated, spends most of its day perched nearby to jealously guard its stash. When another bird dares to filch, the dogfight begins—two miniature prop planes tearing at something near the speed of sound through and around and under—all carried out with an angry buzzing, a domestic quarrel in an alien tongue drunk on helium.

I notice the time. Thirty minutes have passed. There is still a part of me that grates, knowing I cannot provide acceptable justification for spending this chunk of my day.

Not long ago, I attended a writer's workshop in Well, a village on the southeastern border of Holland (near Germany). The workshop took place in a real, honest-to-goodness twelfth-century castle, with genuine moats to protect us from marauders and pillagers. The setting was idyllic, of course, a memorable backdrop for my two-week stay. Sitting by the river, nursing German beer, and watching the barges float by, we swapped stories, fed the insistent ducks, told tall tales, and laughed from the gut.

One evening at dusk I sat alone by the river. The sun was just above the horizon, a dying shimmer. With the harsh light of day dissipated, the contrasting aqua blues and greens of water and foliage melded into four dimensions—lucid and penetrating. I hopped on my bike, and rode by a wall where a villager was finishing her evening gardening chores. I stopped and watched. She held a hand tool and was bent from the waist as she scratched the soil around a lilac shrub, her gestures a mixture of fussing and coddling. She didn't seem to be aware of my presence and went about her business lovingly as if she had all the time in the world. The wall surrounded a rectangular lot, stone walkways through emerald grass patches flanked by borders of late summer blooming hollyhocks and monkshood. It didn't look like any home I'd ever had, but brought tears to my eyes nonetheless, and filled me with a yearning for something deep and still unnamed. For some reason, I felt giddy and alive. I wanted to hug the woman and thank her for the gift.

As I was saying before my detour, we North Americans are not good at waiting for the soul. Or waiting on anything, for that matter. It is no wonder. We reside in a world where living fully means going about your business at a dizzying and distracting pace. We are bombarded with information that ricochets and cascades. We have no time to digest or reflect, and television watching degenerates to television staring. Before you know it, the air is squeezed and stifled with no room for meditation or memories, daydreaming or play. And prayer becomes another channel on an already too crowded band.

Yes, it's easy to be overzealous in this crusade for idleness. I have a predisposition toward sermonizing, like some superhero for the lazy, as if it's essential to convert the wayward. Which suggests to me that it is time to go sink my nose in the confectionery bouquet of our deep lavender bearded iris, just to clear my mind.

For whatever reason, Judith (my wife) and I decide this weekend is as good as any to clear a path. Our driveway takes you down into the canyon, and winds back up to the top of the ridge where our house sits. From our back garden, there is a pathway (now overgrown) which cuts along the ridge and eventually leads down into the canyon where it intersects our drive.

We are woodland militia, armed with loppers and secateurs, and sheathed in clothing to discourage mosquitoes. It is a hot day in late May, so within minutes we are sweaty and tired, blaming one another for hatching this brilliant idea.

After one hundred yards of exertion, we happen upon an area (twenty feet by thirty feet) begging to be extricated and unveiled. We remove a half-dozen alder saplings, trim a thicket of salmonberry, and wrestle with ambitious blackberry vines. With the encasement pulled back, we are welcomed by wondrous surprises. Standing sentry are two seedlings of the oak, *Quercus garryana*. Both are eighteen inches high and fighting for sun. Although the tree is native to the Pacific Northwest, I have not seen a mature Garry oak anywhere near our property—making this offspring a true mystery, our own immaculate conception, which like most true mysteries is best left unsolved.

We happily adopt these orphans and build protective fences with downed hemlock branches. Near the oak trees are two hawthorn seedlings. Also near is a fledgling *Rosa gymnocarpa*, a species rose with airy foliage and petite blooms of bubble-gum pink. Flanking this mix are starts of deciduous and evergreen huckleberry.

The sun is now inviting. We are enveloped in a stillness punctuated by the occasional drumming of a pileated woodpecker. We christen the area as our official picnic glen, and are already planning the next outing when we'll leave the loppers behind, opting for a blanket, mushroom pâté with a loaf of French bread, and a bottle of cabernet.

Georgia O'Keefe once said that "seeing takes time." But this only triggers another part of the problem—that is, our equating time with money and worth. We hear the axiom ("seeing takes time") and obsess, wondering just exactly how much time is required to obtain the prized objective. Our passion is misplaced—like a group of bird watchers on the East Coast who once sponsored a contest with a prize going to the person who could identify the most species in thirty minutes.

Taking time. The very act slowly breaks down the walls we use to separate the sacred from the secular. And allows us to listen. I like Dag Hammarskjöld's observation that "the more faithfully you listen to the voice within you, the better you will hear what is sounding outside. And only he who listens can speak." Which can only happen when we sit. As in "sit for a spell." If we try to make it more, we miss the point, as if sitting is somehow acceptable if we can orchestrate the outcome.

Seeing is another way of talking about being present. We're back to the Sacrament of the Present Moment. Which means that this is as good a time as any to put down the book for awhile, pull up a chair, look out your window, and watch hummingbird theater.

We've heard it argued that embracing idleness is narcissistic. After all, we've only so little time available, so *spending it* means spending it wisely, implying a pace geared toward accomplishment. I've lived that way. But I'm no longer too keen about the return on investment—what, a pat on the back, awards and kudos, recognition as the world's junior messiah?

In his classic study of play, *Homo Ludens,* Johan Huizinga observed that since play is older and more original than civilization, it is fundamentally antithetical to it. This doesn't particularly help us organize our days, but it makes sense. I don't think it means that the two are mutually exclusive, just that we have to keep our antennae up. Which is not an easy thing to do, and is all the more complicated when I watch Martha Stewart—our country's one-woman conglomerate—go about her affairs, done with an enviable air of ease, aplomb, and the appearance of money.

Of course I'm jealous. Watching Martha, it stirs that desire for a simple, unhurried life which is somehow free from drudgery and the manic effort that made it all possible. What is the attraction here? What does she know that we don't? Watching stirs in me that gland which thrives on those twin pillars of worth—busyness and accomplishment—and I measure myself against her achievements while responding to the invitation to be just like her. So I use my Visa card to buy my way into the fraternity, presuming that through osmosis I can become an accomplished gardener, utterly at ease. Who's keeping score now?

The sun passes behind a cloud and the warmth evaporates from my body. I don't know how long I have been napping here. I think of getting on with the task at hand but draw a blank as to what that might be. As if by an electrical switch, the sun reemerges, and a momentary blast of heat rushes through every cell in my body like a welcome intravenous drug. Conroy sneezes and raises his head. I open my eyes to see the white clustered blooms of the 'Kiftsgate' rose above me, wandering through a nearby topped alder. The scent, of allspice, drifts downward. I rack my brain trying to remember what it was I needed to do. I close my eyes and begin to drift off. Whatever it was, it can wait.

# SOUL GARDENING EXERCISES

## *Spend the Afternoon*

Buy a chair. A comfortable chair. A chair that was meant to be lounged in. A chair with your name on it. Put the chair in a place where you can sit for a spell. In the garden or on a porch or out under a tree. Let your thoughts cascade and spill. Give no heed to any compulsion to sort or assess them. And, most importantly, give no heed to the need to justify the time you just gracefully and lavishly "wasted."

Practice the Sacrament of the Present Moment wherever you happen to be now. Lounging on the porch, scrunched in an airplane seat, or sitting in the living room looking at the window sill. Notice details—colors, smells, textures, sounds. Close your eyes and recreate the scene in your mind with as many details as you can remember. Let silence join you.

For one day a week, take off your wristwatch. Deposit it in some unused drawer. If you're lucky, you may forget where you put it. (Then see how many times you catch yourself glancing down at your wrist freckles. And ask yourself why.)

Make a "freedom to loll" date. A time on your calendar to sit still. A "Sabbath" date. I like to call it "Red-X Time." Because such times don't gratuitously appear on my schedule (you know, the "I'll take time when I have time" argument), I must intentionally mark off a time on my schedule with a red X. There's no need to be terribly compulsive about it. Plan for only fifteen minutes. After practice, you can work your way up to several hours! Your options are limitless: lolling in the garden, listening to Bach's "Magnificat," soaking in a hot bath.

How do we perceive time? What does it mean to lose time? To save time?

*Quote for the day: "Millions long for immortality who don't know what to do with themselves on a rainy Sunday afternoon" (Susan Ertz).*

## GREY GATES, NEW EYES

*All of earth is crammed with heaven*
*And every bush a flame with God*
*But only those who see take off their shoes.*
—Elizabeth Barrett Browning

*There is in all things an inexhaustible sweetness and purity, a*
*silence that is a fount of action and joy. It rises up in wordless gentleness*
*and flows out to me from the unseen roots of all created being, welcoming*
*me tenderly, saluting me with indescribable humility.*
—Thomas Merton

For children of all ages, C.S. Lewis's wardrobe has been the entryway to the magical world of Narnia—of emerald witches, talking horses, kings, and magic apples. But for L. R. Holmes of Camp Cottage, Gloucestershire, the threshold to enchantment is nothing more notable than a grey gate. An ordinary grey gate in need of repair.

My companion and I were "on holiday" six miles west of Gloucester in western England, scouring the countryside for private gardens open for tours—each listed in a slim yellow volume we discovered in a timeworn Oxford bookshop. Our day had been carefully planned, an ambitious schedule covering three districts and four gardens. The absence of a speed limit on any motorway accommodated our manic pace. It was mid-afternoon by the time we pulled our car into the Camp Cottage drive. The sight of a lifeless grey gate, flanked by an equally worn, lighter grey, paint-chipped garage was disheartening. If not for a small lemon-colored paper sign—on which was stenciled "GARden TouR SaTURday"—stapled to a tomato stake, we would have chalked it up to a bum map, called it a learning experience, and retired to the nearest pub for solace. Which is never a bad idea.

Instead, slumped behind the wheel on the wrong side of our Vauxhall, I heaved great sighs, and simmered in disappointment.

But . . . beyond the gate.

Caught off guard, my senses reel, unable to fully ingest a Bacchanalian feast. I am greeted by the rambling rose 'Goldfinch,' a prolific and wanton panoply, a twenty-foot tunnel of small salmon-colored blooms, oozing an intoxicating, honeyed sweetness. The pergola on which it spreads, forming an awning over the pathway, is shaped from stout wood staves (each a full six-inch diameter, and made by L. R. and his step-brother "for only 250 pounds sterling," he later reported proudly, with an infectious lack of self-consciousness) and covered prodigally by an intertwining of tawny honeysuckle, milky clematis, and the musky cologne of the antique climbing rose 'Madame Alfred Carriere'—indispensable if for her name only.

From the pergola, a well-worn grass path winds its way to the rustic and medieval cottage door framed by prodigious hand-hewn timbers. On either side of the path, plants jostle and collide.

"I've lived here just seven years," L. R. tells us, conspicuously animated by the sensory banquet around him.

Our guide to Narnia wears understatement as a demeanor. Sixty-five (plus) years of age, longish silver grey hair combed back, ruddy English high cheeks, the beginning of a silver stubble, eyes sparkling behind ordinary black rectangular glasses, and the telltale mark of a gardener (hands worn and rough, with dirt permanently ensconced around the fingernails). L. R. is at home. There is no pretense here. No flaunting. No primping. No air of sophistication with signs around the garden telling you not to touch. I envied L. R. Holmes.

Marcel Proust once wrote that we don't need new landscapes; we need new eyes.

With some 80,000 of my closest friends, I spend a day each February traipsing through the Seattle Convention Center. It is Seattle's renowned "Flower and Garden Show." With the throng I trudge inchmeal, ogling, envying, and marveling at elaborate displays of garden designs and floral artistry. I jot new ideas, and pages of plant names. I see flowers and gadgets I would never use, but cannot live without. (I was unable to say no to the all-in-one rototilling-super-hedge-trimming weed whacker. As far as I know, it is still in the garden shed, anchoring a corner.) I am inspired by the cooling effect of a mass of early spring crocus and leucojum, boggled and covetous of a design with delphinium and English roses blooming in mid-winter and, when the day has ended, I return home with two armloads of literature, advice, and aspirations, needing three full days to recover. Here we go again.

This mixture—equal parts invigoration, appetite, and envy—ferments to a discomfiting froth, awakening the Emma Bovary in me:

> The whole of [my] immediate environment—dull countryside, imbecile petty bourgeois, life in its ordinariness—seemed a freak, a particular piece of bad luck that had seized on [me]; while beyond, as far as the eye could see, ranged the vast lands of passion and fecundity.

Ah yes, Emma, I see those lands, my mind clutches the insidiously beguiling vision—a veritable Ziegfeld Follies—with its leviathan nodding fuchsias, and endless vistas of brazen hyacinths mingled with rainbow-like primroses.

Melodramatic and theatrical, to be sure. But such excess is the occupational hazard for a gardener. A characteristic which blinds us, of course, to the grand irony that extraordinary pockets of wonder—botanical dramas of enchantment—are in, or near, our own back yards.

The flower show amphetamine has run its course, and I recover on my back deck, looking out into the canyon. In the foreground, the white fleur-de-lis blooms of Indian plum have faded, giving way to a delicate, lime green foliage, which carries an ephemeral air. And the creamy panicles on the red elderberry *(Sambucus racemosa)* emerge, upright and resolute as Christmas tree candles. Behind, I see the remaining white cumulus-cloud blooms of our bitter cherry. All of this contrasted by the glossy hunter green of evergreen huckleberry *(Vaccinium ovatum)*. A ruby-throated rufous hummingbird whizzes by on its way to some matter of apparent urgency. And the air is touched with the scent of steamy earth and decomposing leaves. This scene is ubiquitous to our island landscape, so easily unnoticed and taken for granted. For what is familiar to us, our immediate environment, like the girl next door, is seldom fully appreciated or valued.

But it's not just the garden. An old friend calls. We haven't talked in some time. And I'm glad he called. I ask him about his life, and he begins the litany of serendipitous things happening in his world.

I can feel the deflation in my spirit. Instantly certain I can't compete. Although in my head I gave it a whirl, trying to think of some spin on my own story that would make it enviable in its own right, the words stuck somewhere in the back of my throat.

True, we're programmed this way. We can argue that it's a setup, but the result is the same. Beauty is always elsewhere and certainly not beyond the grey gate that marks the entry to my own ordinary world.

Gardening is drudgery. This insight fermented at the age of eleven on a five-acre parcel in southern Michigan. If you wanted tedious, menial, or bothersome work, plant a garden. As in to till, to hoe, and to weed. Especially to weed. These responsibilities fell squarely on my shoulders, the eldest of five.

This charge culminated in my father's consent that I wield our front-tine rototiller (with its 2 1/2 horsepower Briggs and Stratton engine), the model which rattled every bone in your body within thirty seconds, triggering that point of no return when the thrill of being trusted with an adult machine wears off under an abrupt and permanent impact. In rural areas, there's an age of mechanical accountability, when (whether you like it or not) you are old enough to mow the lawn, run a cement mixer, handle a chain saw, and wrestle with a rototiller. Grand illusions fade, as you scheme ways to trade in this birthright you've won. Thank God for younger siblings.

There is no doubt I performed each chore reluctantly, grudgingly, with an eye toward the end of the row, easily a half mile away. It was also evident to me that gardening's unavoidable chores were tasks outside the realm of enjoyment for most adults—something they would not choose to do on their summer vacation but would nonetheless guiltlessly, and with some perverse pleasure, require their children to share in.

"It builds character, son."

From gardening, I learned that character building and fun were, and shall always be, mutually exclusive.

"It'll make a man out of you."

*Man* synonymous with "muscled sweat-stained Neanderthal." And "exhausted."

"When you get to be a parent, you can make your kids pull weeds."

No solace there but, to be honest, I couldn't wait.

Gardening, I deduced, was for ordinary people. And I . . . well, I was to be extraordinary.

As a boy, I lived within the lavish and secure confines of my mind and my dreams, untethered, I hoped, and somehow purified of any sullied affinity to more pedestrian (translate: ordinary and therefore lifeless) investments. For I was a preacher boy—a "chosen one." Preoccupation with matters of nature—and this world—were beneath us devout and philosophical types. When possible, I was a fastidious indoor kid, avoiding unnecessary dirt and soil. I equated time with nature as cavorting with the masses who screeched and frolicked on loud toys. So I was soured to the land by predisposition against those who lived there. By contrast, my mother taught me that I was going to be somebody. And by implication, that meant be somebody someplace other than the place of my childhood. It was a strong and inviolable message that achievement requires no connection with a place. While I have no reason to return, I never realized that in rejecting a way of life, I rejected a piece of my home and of my soul.

May Sarton wrote that we need a way to sanctify the ordinary.

Grey gates and all that.

Which sounds wise, that is, if the ordinary weren't . . . well, so ordinary. We know from experience that ordinary doesn't sell. And no matter how we doctor it up, the fact remains that life is so . . . so, daily.

Everything around us works against sanctifying the ordinary— which is really another metaphor for entering fully into life. (And which stands in contradiction to the mantras of the 1980s—"More is never enough!" and "Who says you can't have it all!"—which may be behind us but are still the sanctioned mottoes for our culture.)

Like most, I have been inculcated in this way of being. One is left with no choice but a manic pace, requiring a plethora of distractions for balance. So we are, by inclination, into "this and that" and forever going "here and there." I am occupied, busy, and weary. Therefore, I am. Hoping, I suppose, to satiate some shape in my soul which cannot be fulfilled, but only compulsively substituted for. It is addictive, to be sure. Aren't we all? But for whatever reason, many of us thrive on wearing a label. So armed with a consumer mentality, we can charge ahead, looking for the product or procedure or self-help book or lottery ticket (or a direct line to God, perhaps?) that will guarantee success, which turns out to be an all too volatile mixture of accumulation, comfort, envy, and ease.

And we find ourselves back with Emma Bovary once again.

But it is not easy to give up our obsession with new landscapes, as if this is some genetic right for the American pioneer.

To see with new eyes requires us to stop. And to sit down. And suspend our distractions. But, to stop is easier said than done.

"I'm going to be fifty-nine soon, and some day I'd like to be able to stroll down Union Street and spend the afternoon window shopping." Those were some of the first words spoken by a client of psychiatrist Irvin Yalom. They struck a chord with De Yalom, and after the session, he mused, "I know all about the longing to take a noonday stroll. How many times have I yearned for the luxury of a carefree Wednesday afternoon walk through San Francisco? Yet, I have continued to work compulsively and to impose a professional schedule on myself that makes that stroll impossible. I knew we were both chased by the same man with a rifle."

Being chased is quintessential Americana. We're nursed on the milk of great expectations, of dreams and potential. And our life course follows a prescribed route, which is all well and good until one day when the gears grind to a halt, and you wonder what the hell you're doing on *this* pathway instead of *that*. Which leads to the distraction of direction, and we still miss the point.

I was predisposed to find grey distasteful or, at the very least, wanting. And the word *ordinary* sits acidic in my mouth. Isn't it odd that we take it all so very personally, as if *ordinary* is an indictment no less, and our very identity is at stake.

L. R. Holmes designed his cottage garden in a way that requires one to loll and meander, to stop and stare, and to unwittingly get soused on fragrance. Clever devil. Even English gardens serve bliss by the pint. But then English cottage gardens are like that, places of romance where the imagination can flower. A world of magic and delight—of wide-eyed wonder.

Exploration is a given. I needed to walk the narrow grass path around each border or pergola to see the surprise that waited on the other side. I admit it, I could not keep in check the spontaneous rush of adrenaline that is triggered by fascination and the reality of limitation. Like a child in a candy store, I explored from counter to counter, display to display, my appetite alive. I was filled with awe, wonderment, hunger, and sadness, knowing full well that my capacity to devour it all was wishful thinking.

I can admit it now. On that day, I fell hard. Head over heels hard. I fell in love with a cottage garden. (Cottage gardens are a tradition begun in England out of necessity where small spaces needed to accommodate the need to grow food, herbs, and flowers—rosemary, sage, lupine, mallow, and aster—with no dividing line between flower garden and vegetable patch.) In this case, it is a full-acre, seventeenth-century cottage garden. It surrounds a Cromwellian cottage that resembles some hideaway from the Hobbit, with its thatched roof perched high like a bad toupee. "With the original thatch roof intact," L. R. informed us. "In fact, Cromwell himself actually used this cottage as a headquarters during the war." With his English inflection, *war* was amended into a command needed to stop a horse and carriage.

There is a Chinese proverb which says that to be happy for a week you take a new concubine, to be happy for a month you kill a pig, and to be happy all your life you build a garden. I can't vouch for the first two, but the last is true.

Happiness has always been one of those red flag words for me. I can relate to Meg Tilly's character in the movie *The Big Chill* who says, "I haven't met that many happy people in my life. How do they act?" And those who profess happiness seem to be conspicuously withholding some part of the story.

Even so, there's something to be said for people who live happily for reasons that elude the sophisticated sciences of our pop-psychology culture. It appears there are those who, for lack of a better option or for want of a better explanation, simply enjoy life. I've never done a scientific survey to verify the results of the proverb's assertion, but I can vouch for L. R. Holmes. He, too, agrees with the Chinese proverb.

For two hours my companion and I immersed ourselves into the mosaic of color and the jumble of scents that was L. R.'s garden. Beguiled by the mock orange *Philadelphus* 'Belle Étoile' decked in pristine white and bestowing its clean citrus perfume on any who pass by. Magnetized by a mishmash of textures, the narrow lime green leaves of *Penstemon glaber,* covered with a fluorescent cobalt flower, sharing space with the erect spires of a campanula, extending its paper-thin amethyst bell-like flowers, and the needled pungency of rosemary.

Well, there was simply no alternative. Extreme emotions call for extreme measures. So. I sat down for some time. On a bench near the garden edge, sharing the seat with a drowsy and placid cat, I let the sunshine work its antidote. It's not easy, to just sit. I wanted to be productive in my sitting. I wanted to describe what I was seeing, what I was feeling. I wanted to find the right words or take a picture, wanting to find a container for this moment.

Before long, the internal manic cadence begins to lose its steam. And your eyes begin to refocus. Off come the shoes, and you settle in, to revel in the gift. And on this afternoon, you pretend to be characters in some Victorian novel, enjoying tea under the pergola, served by butlers, no less, and serenaded with the continuous hum of bees busily absorbed in honeysuckle and delphinium. On this afternoon, you play guessing games with white cloud shapes, and relish the buoyant blue sky and the lavish waste of time. For there is something about the whole experience that provokes a replay of the lazy summer afternoons of childhood, laying belly-up under the apple tree, grass stem in mouth, a remembrance of the time when one unquestionably expected fantasies would come true and when ordinary wardrobes did indeed lead to the land of Narnia.

It has to do with L. R.'s grey gate, I told myself. So, I took copious mental notes. I wanted to race home and create a replica garden, to piggyback on L. R.'s happiness. If it is Narnia, after all, who wants to go back to the same old home? More likely, we find a passion and drain it of every last ounce of joy. And we miss the point.

No matter. I still wanted the formula.

Then one day it happens. When you are wandering the back border of the garden for a better look at the western tanager perched in a neighboring hemlock, or seduced by the fragrance of the Asiatic lily, 'Casablanca,' or enchanted by the filigree starts of bronze fennel, or even battling an encroaching and overly opportunistic red elderberry. It hits you, like a flare in your frontal lobe, that you have no image to defend here, and that the rules you've spent your life so meticulously preserving are for naught. All you can do is grab a chair and mull it over for awhile—it occurs to you that there is no assignment due, so you decide to dance around the wild geraniums and gooseneck loosestrife with your black Lab Conroy (who suspects brain damage but indulges you nonetheless) just for the hell of it.

And you catch yourself hoping that no one was watching. After all, what will they think? It's not easy to shake, this predisposition to obsess and protect an image. I've carried the disease throughout most of my adult life, looking over my shoulder just to see who's taking notes. Some hangover from my youth when it was vital not to offend anyone. Which makes this an issue of boundaries. An odd word in a culture where we consume in order to find ourselves.

Truth is, it is difficult to celebrate small delights. It is difficult to "waste" time looking at grey gates. Which makes this invitation to new eyes, or enter fully into life, all the more necessary.

Recently, I had the pleasure of visiting the gardens of Arthur "Art" Kruckeberg, botanist, professor, husband, apologist, and guru of Northwest native plants. The Kruckeberg garden and nursery occupies four-plus acres in the middle of one of Seattle's north shore suburbs, an oddity for its size and its stand of second-growth conifers. I say garden, but it is more accurately an arboretum, with striking specimens of trees ranging from northern California oak to the white-fringed silver fir *(Abies amabilis)*. It is a garden. And it is a playground. Art, still tall and straight shouldered in his seventy-sixth year, carries a European demeanor, accented with longish white-silver hair and matching grey-silver goatee. With his pipe in hand and French beret aslant on his head,

Art escorts us around, telling plant stories, Ciceronian and loquacious, giddy as a schoolboy with a new treat.

"Look at that foliage," he effusively points to a cut-leafed Tan oak, its foliage as incised as a lumberman's saw. "Isn't it wonderful?" New eyes indeed. Ever the advocate for these native "children," Art is not merely our tour guide. He is an evangelist. He sincerely hopes this walking homily can heal the sick and make the near-blind see. When you see the burning bush and take off your shoes, you risk giving up control, a sure cause of much of our blindness.

I read somewhere that it would not hurt us to loosen our control and allow a "modicum of floral anarchy." Off our back deck is a typical island understory. Clumps of huckleberry (deciduous and evergreen), some scattered red currant shoots, clusters of Oregon grape, a large *Holodiscus* shrub, willow saplings, and madrone. The scene is flanked by a grouping of towering western hemlocks. In this tangle of verdancy, plants comingle and intertwine, a scene tousled and disheveled. It had been my original hope to clear, as in bulldoze, much of the area for a more appropriate, as in tidy, landscaping. I saw some plans somewhere that would have been perfect.

Indeed. It is *the* temptation. In his book *The Country Garden*, John Brookes illuminates our condition:

> The pollution of the countryside is not only a matter of nitrates and silage effluent, of urban sprawl and brightly lit petrol stations; a far more subtle contamination comes from tidiness. The obsessive and contagious mania for suburban conformity reaches out into rural habitats. Mown verges, white chains and swinging name-boards are seeping down the lanes. Plants acquired by the car-load from the invidious garden-center are placed with the precision of pieces on a chessboard.

Tidiness now sounds more like a disease.

In the end, we did not clear the area. We let it go, save for plucking out a few overly ambitious alder and hemlock seedlings and removing the spent fronds of last year's bracken fern. This past fall, a pileated woodpecker decided to honor the "back deck garden," attaching himself to a huckleberry shrub for lunch. His weight made for an awkward posture: the branch bent, his body tilted. He lunched contentedly while I watched and gave thanks that I hadn't had my way.

There's a winsome Hasidic story about a Rabbi Itsak, son of Yekel, who lived in eastern Europe and received instructions in a dream to travel a great distance to a castle where he would find a buried treasure. Eagerly, he covered the many miles. Upon his arrival, he befriended a castle guard and, without telling his name, told the details of his dream.

The guard laughed and laughed. "So you wore out all your shoe leather just to please a silly dream? If I had as much faith as you, I would have journeyed to Prague where my dream told me to go to the house of a Rabbi Itsak, son of Yekel, where a treasure is buried under his stove."

Rabbi Itsak thanked the guard and hurried home. There, under the floor planks near his stove, he discovered a buried treasure.

There is, no doubt, a temptation to go overboard here. Almost a cliché—be thankful for who you are, and all that. But that's not quite it, either. I can start to tell you where to look and what to see, and we're off the mark altogether.

Either you see it or you don't, which isn't much good to someone looking for directions. But then again, if you are looking for happiness with such ardor, it would not hurt to take a day off and dance in the geraniums.

Who cares what they think?

After all, it's your garden.

My friend was in the process of writing a book on parenting. He asked his two small sons, "Boys, how do you know Dad loves you?"

He figured that they would say, "Dad, we knew you loved us when you took us to Disney World for, like, ten days." They didn't say that, and he knew he had wasted that money.

He figured they would say, "Dad, we knew you loved us when you bought us all those Christmas presents." They didn't say that, either.

They said, "Dad we know you love us when you wrestle with us."

He remembers twice when he had come home late, tired and disinterested, and these two urchins were jerking on his pants. He told me, "I rolled with them on the floor toward the kitchen just to get them out of my way. And in the middle of that very ordinary, mundane event, real life was happening. Real life. But I missed it, because I was only tuned in to Disney World and Christmas."

New eyes. Sanctifying the ordinary takes place in those dollops of time as we putter and futz, and flit and hope. Mirabel Osler, in her book *Gentle Plea for Chaos,* talks about the art of squandering slivers of time. Which means that today there is no timetable. No pressing schedule.

I have a hunch that L. R. Holmes wouldn't think much of my musings on happiness. If there is a correlation between gardening and happiness, it is certainly not intentional. He, like Osler, is one of those "improper" gardeners. Gardening, that is, for the sheer love of it.

I mention to L. R. that it is a pleasure to spend some time with a rose and perennial expert. "Oh," he sounds surprised, caught off guard, "I'm only a dedicated amateur," followed by a self-effacing shrug, a quick smile, and a laugh. He found any thought of his being a professional or an expert unthinkable.

Gardening for the sheer love of it. For the thrill of the translucent shimmer as the afternoon sun strikes the light pink petals of a 'Cécile Brünner' rose bud. The physical pause one feels at first sight of the blood red blooms from the 'Bishop of Llandaff' dahlia. The vivid lavender of top-heavy delphinium spires against a wall of the delicate white rose, 'Celeste.' And the gratifying and bracing aroma of the early summer English roses—'Perdita' and 'Othello.'

Such lavish waste.

Happiness, it appears, is an afterthought, the obsession of a culture seeking self-fulfillment. A subject for essayists like me—those of us who find comfort simmering in our Vauxhalls. But for L. R. Holmes of Camp Cottage, it is enough to flit and amble, to dig and savor, to plant and nurture, to fret and coddle.

I watch L. R. potting some cuttings of a woody penstemon. I watch his hands. Hands that know soil, and plants by name, feel, touch. Hands weathered by use, yet gentle and nimble and caring, able to work with the fragile shoot of a rare sweet pea. He takes some cuttings from two or three of the perennials I had admired. "Here," he hands them to me, "keep these in some damp sphagnum, for your Seattle garden."

Sanctify the ordinary.

I am struck by the rootedness that comes with investment. Literally giving a damn. For time, energy, devotion, and care will root you. You are connected to the earth. Imprinted by the ordinary particularity of it all. This plot. This place. This time. This season—come hell or high water. You fight the elements and nature. You face disappointment and loss and grief. You learn to repair and hope and forgive.

And you try again.

And you watch.

And you nurture.

And you drink in the lavish repayment of investment in the form of this brief slice of heaven.

"I'm retired," L. R. adds to a conversation that has ebbed and flowed through the various pathways. He pauses, "Besides, this is what I want to do."

A bit further down the path he stops, shakes his head, and chuckles, "And some people wonder why I spend all my time gardening. But I say to them, why not? Why not do what I really want to do at this age?"

Why not indeed?

And he's off again, to another side of a mixed border, around a corner—or a grey gate—where more enchantments await, eagerly and proudly displaying their objet d'art on a canvas washed in honey-mustard yellow, drizzled with lustrous shades of midnight blue.

# SOUL GARDENING EXERCISES

## Grey Gates, New Eyes

Sanctifying the ordinary may mean nothing more than pondering the mundane. (Nicholson Baker can write an entire book around one mundane moment, such as a young father's afternoon reverie as he sits in his child's nursery room.) But sanctifying the mundane takes practice. Choose an ordinary event in your day. Intentionally stop what you are doing and notice the details. Touch textures, be aware of smells, listen to sounds, entertain memories that are evoked.

Think back to your youth. (It may take an effort for some of us.) Think about your worlds of wonder from your childhood. What did those worlds look like? And how did you get there?

Take a backyard tour—of your own backyard. Look again at the sagging plant in the clay pot, the hedge that needs trimming, the place under the shrubbery where the cat curls for her nap. Now look again through a child's eyes. The overgrown shrub becomes a secret fort. . . .

If you have a garden space, share it with a friend, or a child, a senior citizen, a person with a disability, a person who has no garden. Enjoy the garden through their eyes.

Get up early one morning and listen to the dawn.

*Quote for the day:"If you pass by the color purple in a field and don't notice it, God gets real pissed off"(Alice Walker).*

# SUMMER

---

*To be intoxicated with the world around us . . .*
*To live passionately with no holds barred*

# THREE

## MOMENTS OF INTOXICATION

*Life without moments of intoxication is not worth "a pitcher of spit."*
—Kurt Vonnegut

*A healthy child has no interest in persons; he in interested in things.*
*When a child is sure of his mother's love, he forgets his mother; he goes*
*out to explore the world; he is curious. He looks for a frog to put in his*
*mouth—this kind of thing.*
—Anthony de Mello

We are standing near the gate of an English cottage. A stone's throw away, we can see and hear the stream that drifts and surges through the quaint Oxfordshire village of Bibury. Near the gate, branches from a purple Smoke Bush enfold mounds of Lady's Mantle, leaves of tawny port melded with floral sprays of chartreuse, scattered on pillows of muted lime green. The jolt from this montage discharges directly at the brain stem, coursing through the nervous system. This is, after all, a drug ingested sensually, its impact swift and rudimentary.

A Cotswold stone wall encircles the plot. From the wooden green gate, a path leads to the cottage door. On either side of the path, plants jostle one on top of the other. Plants packed together, serving as their own stakes, support one another like drunks after a party.

This is gardening—this is life—no holds barred. Anything goes. There are no tidy rows, no recommended spacing, no unwelcome surprise guests. This is gardening brimming to excess. Gardening that engenders an intimacy born of mingling and fraternizing. Blades of bearded iris jut through clumps of the wild geranium 'Kashmir Purple.' Mounds of *Cheiranthus,* like Tory wigs hanging from pegs, spill out of invisible cracks in the Cotswold stone. Nothing is cerebral or contrived. There is no need to be sophisticated, ingenious, or trendy. There is, after all, no image to defend.

Near the road outside of the wall stands an iron cart overcrowded with potted plants—seedlings and cuttings from the garden's overflow. On the cart is a box for our money. One to two pounds sterling per plant, the honor system. I have difficulty making up my mind, fretting about the amount of space left in the car. Still hedging, I place coins in the box for three plants.

I was raised in a world where *excess* is a dirty word. I assimilated and absorbed life in the school of antiseptic gardening, requiring, even demanding, a well-mannered, well-modulated world. That is, all things in their correct places. Above all, tidy and evenly spaced, with no threat of overflow, for there nothing touches. I chose to strive for what was proper and tasteful. Unobtrusive and correct. In this light, my vocational choice made sense. The thought of intoxication as a prerequisite for my soul was utter heresy!

I excelled (cum laude and all that) in the school where image is everything, measured against the requirement to do things "correctly." So it is no surprise that all areas of my life were carefully scripted. At the same time, my Midwestern religious heritage taught me to never feel prideful or exuberant of possessions or skills or accomplishments. So I kept all of my emotions in check, meting out only those that I or others deemed appropriate. I went overboard protecting myself against the sin of immoderation.

Avoiding the pit of being at the mercy of my feelings, that discomfiting place where passions rage and demons howl, where colors bubble and explode, where one is no longer in control, no longer restrained, as the heart—not to be trusted—wildly races. For incentive, and to stay the course of control, I carried in my mind pictures of men with puffed scarlet faces, contemptible and pitied. I was above that, surely. And the result is that there was a part of myself, this cauldron of passions, I entombed. Of what was I afraid?

Your guess is as good as mine. However you slice it, there is, to be sure, a price to be paid for living this way—all emotions restricted, close to the chest. The payoff is certainly for the short run, while we still enjoy the apparent rewards for our protectiveness, as the world feels manageable and comfortable. Meanwhile, our enemies—our fears—are kept at bay by true grit.

But down the road, something snaps. While I sit on the back deck, the sun sets over the Kitsap Peninsula (the expanse of land west of Seattle and Puget Sound). The sky, as if batter poured from a pitcher, turns an effluence of slate blue and vermilion. Spires of hemlock are backlit and silhouetted like hand puppets on an immense screen. I stand for some unknown reason, singing, "Jeremiah was a bullfrog. Was a good friend of mine. . . ." at the top of my lungs, and do a little boogie with my dog, who hasn't the foggiest idea what's come over me but is a sucker for a party and plays along nonetheless. I let the moment melt around me before I gain my composure and give myself some sort of reality check: a quiz requiring justification for what I'm feeling and why. And then it hits me. I can't tell a soul about my dance at twilight without coming face-to-face with who I was pretending not to be and the energy it required to maintain that image.

When I lived in Southern California, I spent three days a month at a Benedictine monastery out in the high desert. It was my periodic trek to a place where I could slow down long enough to pay attention. Truth is, I wanted to learn how to be alone with myself and like it, because I wasn't very good at that. And, I wanted to learn how to be alone with God and like it, because I wasn't very good at that, either.

On one visit, a friend asked one of the monks, "What exactly do you do here?"

"We pray," the monk replied simply.

"No," my friend persisted, "I mean besides that. What do you really do?"

"It is enough just to pray," the monk told my friend.

"It is enough," I tell my dog standing on the deck absorbing the summer sky, "just to boogie." Just to boogie under the inexplicable marbled canopy of dusk. Just to feel your lungs swell and your heart flutter. Just to cheer the sun as it sets and not give a damn about some need to fight back the tears, standing spellbound in the salty prism for twilight rainbows.

I recently visited a friend's garden in a Seattle neighborhood. Betty's in the vicinity of eighty years, but I don't ask. Her life story reads like an outlandish quest. She lived for some years on a small fishing boat in Alaska (on which she raised her children) and is now settled in her Seattle home with her three or four cats. She reads and putters, writes and tends her garden, a backyard garden maybe forty feet by seventy feet. Like a store of whimsical and stray potpourri, the space is crammed to the gills. Over there, on a small patio of old brick pavers, makeshift benches stand gilded with clay pots, spilling herbs and various seedling surprises. Betty makes no effort to evict these unexpected boarders, but welcomes them with open arms.

We pass a Greek oregano plant, standing alone in one little pot. The plant lists from the weight of a decided sag. She explains its condition, brushing her hand against the plant. "I need to touch it every time I go by. Here," she urges me, pulling off a leaf and raising it to my nose, "you need to smell this."

Around a mock orange shrub near the back of the lot are raised beds full of vegetables—string beans, carrots, lettuce, and tomatoes. Wedged between them and the wall, three or four raspberry bushes scramble toward the sun. There is just barely enough room on the pathway, as plants from both sides encroach and overflow. A rose wanders up the side of the garage.

"Come over here," she directs me to behind the small garage. In a shaded area is a bench made of stout tree branches. "It's my solitude seat," she tells me. "Whenever I want to be alone, I can come out here and sit in my secret spot, and nobody knows where I am."

I read somewhere that your garden doesn't have to be Eden, it just has to be your own little slice of heaven. Indeed. Fortunately, it never occurred to Betty whether she had done it "right." Betty is a true gardener, happy as only the obsessed can be.

Of course, writing about intoxication blunts the moment, as now it must be weighed, measured, evaluated. There's that part of us that needs to bottle up what we've got or discovered. In the same way that we take pictures on our vacation, I suppose, so we can capture the moment for some weary night after the years have bleached the memories. The upshot, more often than not, is that we are so focused on acquiring the photo, we miss the very reason we were mesmerized to begin with.

There is a rule of thumb for any writer wannabe. Just write. Glue your butt to the chair, and write. And then write some more. Begin by writing without appraisal. Let it flow—even if only in fits and starts, regardless of its value or merit or worth. Put it down on the page. Without stopping to judge or rethink or spell check. In due time. In due time.

It's the same rule of thumb for the gardener. Paint the landscape in your mind. Let plants cascade and jumble. With paths and walls and waterways. Embrace plants from your childhood—and plants from your dreams. Give no heed to "I can't" or "I shouldn't."

When people visit my garden, they ask for advice on their own backyard Shangri-las. Some are starting from scratch. Others are working with a garden they have had for years. Some have lots of space. Others have two or three whiskey barrels on their patio.

"There's always room for one more plant," is my best advice, stealing from Oscar Wilde's reflection, "Nothing succeeds like excess." Of course, once given the opportunity to dispense such acumen, I decide not to stop. The preacher in me is in full gear. "Besides," I tell them, "Good taste is definitely overrated. Because you can't really make a mistake in the garden. Honestly, if you don't like the way something turns out, you can always move it in the fall or early spring. That's part of the fun, and the wonder." Which is about the time I usually spot some clump of an unnamed aster that has run amok, doing my best to resist the urge to starting whacking at it with a spade.

"Experimenting," I exhort, spurred on by the choir in my mind, "that's gardening at its best. Moving things around, and seeing the combinations create mosaics you couldn't have imagined. Of course some of them are garish. Some of them might even bring tears to your eyes." I notice a patch of an exotic-looking salvia that has appropriated a corner of my own garden. I make a mental note about escorting it elsewhere and continue, "So be it. Think of it as a teenager going through some phase. One more thing: never, ever consider yourself finished." I feel a bit like Churchill now, repeating for emphasis with my best British accent, "Nevah. Nevah. Nevah."

Therein lies the temptation. As if we can ultimately "get it right." I guess a part of us doesn't mind giving in to some form of excess, as long as it is time constrained. (Like my friend who tells me, "Of course I'm spontaneous, just me tell me which day, so I can put it on my calendar.") We know there will be some hour or place when we will be done with this madness. Project over. And we give thanks to whomever may be responsible, for the order in our world is restored.

It's not easy, as I said, being in a world where *excess* is still a dirty word. There's the rub. It's difficult to argue for moments of intoxication in a world where intoxication splits families and destroys lives.

Even so, we're very big on addiction in this culture. Everyone I know is "in recovery," or has done stints "in recovery," from one fixation or another. Lord knows I've had my share of self-induced, dizzying bouts with addictive excess, triggering cycles of self-pity, rage, and self-hatred. It's not unusual for us clergy types. It's not the collar, but the climate with which we have been surrounded, demanding circumspect behavior on the one hand and a complete intolerance of personal failure on the other. The result, sooner or later, is a split personality or, at the least, exhaustion.

There have been times of addictive behavior in my life where I have been duly ashamed and frightened—enough to generate a kick in the tail to marshal all of my will power, each time making promises to walk the straight and narrow and never stumble again. Gritting my teeth, I have lived life on a razor's edge, keeping at bay whatever gnawed my soul but able to report to the unseen panel of judges that "I stood firm and didn't give in." I was, to be sure, in control. Which is another great example of winning the battle and losing the war. It makes you wonder who decided that life and health is all about control and restraint, anyway.

When we were young, we saw the good life as a letting go, living to the hilt. We were, of seeming necessity, out of control.

But now we're a culture coming clean. Coming to terms with our propensity toward addiction. And excess. So the pendulum swings, as we disown anything that smacks of fixation, shunning obsession, paring our life down to the basics, now measured and fueled by self-control. Becoming, with little irony, all the more fixated and obsessed. To which Kurt Vonnegut writes:

> To all my friends and relatives in Alcoholics Anonymous, I say that they were right to become intoxicated. Life without moments of intoxication is not worth "a pitcher of spit," as the felicitous saying goes. They simply chose what was for them a deadly poison on which to get drunk.
>
> Good examples of harmless toots are some of the things children do. They get smashed for hours on some strictly limited aspect of the Great Big Everything, the Universe, such as water or snow or mud or colors or rocks (throwing little ones, looking under big ones), or echoes or funny sounds from the voice box or banging on a drum and so on. The child does a little something to the Universe, and the Great Big Everything does something funny or beautiful or sometimes disappointing or scary or even painful in return. The child teaches the Universe how to be a good playmate, to be nice instead of mean.

There is no sedative strong enough to eradicate the sounds and smells of a country childhood. My family did not own a farm, although fertile farmland surrounded us. Each spring the air was generously perfumed with the bouquet of fresh cow manure. Like most rural homes, however, we planted a garden—meaning only one thing in ruralese: a vegetable garden. Our plot was sizable, even for a country garden, measuring 60 feet by 120 feet. In the return visits of my adult years, while everything else—barn, house, backyard baseball diamond—has diminished in size, that garden plot still stands portentous, larger than life. When I was young, summer found it engorged with melons, pumpkins, potatoes, onions, beets, carrots, lettuce, and sweet corn—our own supermarket produce aisle—with an additional border of asparagus, clumps of rhubarb, and a patch of raspberry bushes.

One of my chores was planting sweet corn, using an ingenious contraption one might now find in the dusty corner of an overlooked antique store. Today, it would surely evoke a crinkled brow and amused scrutiny, followed by a predictable, "What in tarnation is that thing?" That "thing" consisted of a pole, one end resembling the duck-billed blades on a posthole digger. Atop the blades sat a can—an ordinary coffee can—that held the sweet-corn seed. The blades were inserted into the soil and, in the same motion, the pole was shoved forward. This motion opened the soil while activating a spring attached to a slotted cogwheel joined at the bottom of the can, which methodically moved one notch, releasing a single kernel into the trough.

Planting sweet corn was the one and only task my siblings and I fought over. Monotony and routine had not yet blunted our curiosity, and we were not beyond digging up each kernel just to make sure it had been planted. Until my father hollered at us, we could easily replant the same kernel over a dozen times.

The north side of the garden was flanked by a grape arbor, almost fifty feet in length. They were Concord grapes, plump and murky. On your way by, you took a grape between thumb and forefinger, squeezing the pulp from its leathery jacket into your mouth. It was, and still is, the drug of choice on a hot July day.

I remember the stains in the cheese cloth, and on our clothes, from our annual juicing, putting away endless dozens of mason jars in the cellar. Once juiced, however, the allure was gone, as the liquid underwent a subtle transformation—becoming a drink to be ingested under great duress, due to its unmistakable association with our Baptist church communion wine and the accompanying, obligatory, browbeating sermon. This stain of religious damnation and woe is as indelible as the inky birthmark left by spilled Concord grape juice.

There's something fundamentally unnerving about living life so fully awake. So I find myself wanting to put the kibosh on the no-holds-barred part of me. Instead, I keep it in check, make no mistakes, and avoid being the fool.

I see now that the whole issue of intoxication has been turned on its head. As adults we can forget that we entered this world wired to get high on the "solid, nutritious food of life—namely, work, play, fun, laughter, the company of people, the pleasure of the senses and the mind." But from an early age, A. S. Neill reminds us, "[we] were given a taste for the drug called approval, appreciation, attention. . . . Having a taste for these drugs, we become addicted and began to dread losing them."

The result? We drug ourselves with anything that we hope will compensate for the drug of life itself. This, of course, is terribly difficult to do with a flower, unless you're fond of using a weed whacker, and you're bent on restraint—gardening with a very heavy hand, tidy and precise.

An invitation to be "smashed for hours on some strictly limited aspect of the Great Big Everything," or even "harmless toots," is intimidating when you are expecting life to be a transaction which requires a payoff—living in the shadow of some balance sheet, detailing what is owed and what is past due. There's no doubt that we are a formula-oriented culture, and we want to know the steps. In this case, the saying is true: Life always happens when your head is turned. Like when the sun is just above the trees and the sky begins its early-evening kaleidoscope, and the scorecards simply make no sense.

Vonnegut goes on to say that the game is only played well with two, namely, the child and the Universe. As adults, we allow the inclusion of a third party with the power to judge and ridicule and grade. He's got a point there. It's our repression of excess that has helped land us in this mess to begin with. And our insides remain a cauldron of anger with no outlet.

Our desire, or need, to keep the world tidy and nice presupposes a requirement for looking away from those parts of ourselves that embarrass or confuse or mortify. If there's a dark side, we think it is best to keep it under wraps, forgetting that such repression requires fuel. We find ourselves living secret lives, medicated by this or that to avoid the myriad feelings that assuage and cascade when the valves are left wide open.

Or maybe that third person is in the confines of our mind, making sure that we toe the line, keep from straying. There is something frightening about stepping outside the line. Even "in recovery" we find ways to keep score.

There will always be those who step outside the line for shock value, marshaling some feeble argument about the nobility of their cavalier recklessness, an odd mixture of desperately needing the attention while telling the world where to get off.

With irony, such an individual is in the same fix as the one rendered immobile from fear. Both are, it seems to me, suffering from an excessive dose of self-consciousness. Both are feeling the glare of that third party in their heads demanding that they dance to one particular tune, or else. Some of us capitulate and dance. Some of us snap and kill the music, all the while looking over our shoulders just to see if *they* noticed.

Like it our not, it is our spirituality at stake. The part of us that makes us fully human—the gardener in us—with the capacity to revel in the wonder of life, takes a turn for the awkward when we invite any third party on our journey. We miss the point that our spiritual nature is enhanced precisely when, for precious moments, we are able to shake that voice and find ourselves knee-deep in the colors, smells, and emotions of the day.

Spirituality pushes us deeper and deeper into our existence. Genuinely intoxicated—this man and his dog, boogying under the marbled canopy of dusk—reveling in the wonders, the solid, nutritious food of life.

Whenever I visit anyone's home, I wander around the yard or land or patio, looking for plants and surprises. I always plunge my hands into the soil, to smell it, squeeze it—drawing puzzled and mystified stares.

"What in the hell are you doing?" one friend asked, embarrassed, when he found me digging around at the home where we had gone for a social gathering.

"Talking to the dirt," I told him.

"How many drinks have we had?" he asked with a smile reserved for unruly children.

Then it occurred to me: you have to be a little looped to be a good gardener. You see the world askew from most folks. But it's an advantage. And besides, the alternative—to be frozen by public opinion—isn't so good.

I read a story about a boy who was asked by his grade school teachers if he wanted to play a part in the Christmas nativity play. Well, of course he did. "Good," the teacher told him. "You get to be Joseph."

The boy was proud, what with his friends having to be sheep and cows and such. "What are my lines?" he asked.

"You don't have any," the teacher answered.

"But what do I do?" the boy asked.

"You just stand there," the teacher said, "and make sure Mary doesn't look bad."

The boy did just that. Standing frozen throughout the entire play. After it was over, adults patted him on the head and told him, "You were such a marvelous Joseph." And he was proud.

The boy grew up and wondered, "If I was such a marvelous Joseph, why did I never once talk to Mary? If I was such a marvelous Joseph, why did I never once pick up the baby Jesus and sing him a song? If I was such a marvelous Joseph, why did I never once offer coffee to the shepherds? I was a marvelous Joseph only because I did what everyone said I should do. I was marvelous because I was frozen."

Frozen Joseph. And your insides grind to a halt, wound tight and immobile. Frozen Joseph. And your garden becomes an unsullied landscape designed for drive-by viewing.

Frozen Joseph.

I had a priest friend tell me about his church nativity play. A young girl, playing the part of the innkeeper, needed to respond to Mary and Joseph's question, "Is there any room in the inn?" As the Bible's rendition goes, the innkeeper replies, "No. There is no room in the inn." But this little girl paused as she looked at Mary and Joseph. She looked out at the priest and at her parents. She looked again at Mary and Joseph and told them, "You might as well at least come in for a drink or two."

Ah yes, exuberance rears its wonderfully scandalous head.

Today the wind is coming out of the south, a summer squall, whipping and swirling, on edge and high-strung. The sky somersaults and lurches. It surges and tumbles. Sitting in our house atop a knoll, we see the whole landscape in motion and unsettled. Nothing feels fixed. There is no anchor.

The bank of clouds to the west is a horizontal rainbow, painted with laminations of pink and rose and ruby. To the north, storm clouds hover as if by magnet—robing the Sound with vast sheets of grey gauze like curtains for the show. This is nature's grand excess—exuberance on display.

The air is charged, stirring the soul like some Tchaikovsky symphony. Cymbals crashing. Tympanis rumbling. Cannons booming. You are on your feet for this one. The music pulsates through your blood. There is life in this storm, life unmitigated and unencumbered. And you want to be permeated and washed with its potency and mettle.

The garden, as always, loses the battle with this wind and rain, and slumps, worse for wear. Lavatera 'Barnsley' branches are snapped, Shasta Daisies splayed, delphinium spikes broken. Serene vistas are shot to hell.

Yet, it is the price to be paid.

Therein lies another conundrum—face-to-face with whether or not we truly wish to live in the arena of excess. I'll admit that I have never been big on excess or gusto. I was reared with an automatic censor, a meter designed to modify or delete or purge. Reminders from my childhood periodically tumble through my mind.

"What do you think you're doing?"

"Why don't you settle down? Now!"

"Let's don't get carried away."

"There's no need to go overboard." All essential waivers for the insecure part of me.

Yes. There is a price to be paid. Beginning with the admittance to a world where predictability and comfort is subservient to extravagance and intoxication.

Calvin, from the comic strip "Calvin and Hobbes," is my role model here. "Wow," he tells Hobbes, "look at the grass stains on my skin. I say, if your knees aren't green by the end of the day, you ought to seriously reexamine your life!"

My wife and I walk down by the river that runs through this quaint English village of Bibury. We have crossed the road from the iron cart and have deposited our three new plants in the "boot" of our rental car. The area alongside the river has been set aside as a bird and wildlife sanctuary, and the stream is home to several new families. We have taken a keen interest in a pair of spirited coots. Over the three weeks of our vacation, we've stopped by to see how the eggs are hatching. We sit on the stone ledge to watch. A coot nest rests on the water near the edge of the stream, anchored by sticks and grass debris—a floating atoll, its own garden of exceptional lavishness. Over the three-week period, five young birds have hatched. Only two have survived. We fret over their loss, and wonder why the world contains the inevitability of such disappointment.

Both mom and dad are on unremitting feeding duty, shuttling back and forth from the nest with tidbits for the ever eager chicks. There is no recess in their enthusiasm. I watch. I absorb.

And as I watch, I decide to cross back over the road to the iron cart with a few more coins in hand, confident that this time two dozen plants are not nearly enough.

# SOUL GARDENING EXERCISES

## *Moments of Intoxication*

I'd tell you to go boogie with your dog under the canopy of dusk, but the effect would smack of rules and regulations. Even so, give it a whirl.

Remember picking that first plump strawberry fresh from the vine, wiping the flecks of dirt away, tasting the mixture of the sun's warmth and the sweetness of the fruit as it literally melted in your mouth? There are few experiences in life as sensuous, as close to ecstasy. . . .

Ask yourself what it is about our culture that fears such ecstasy—that is, ecstasy that is not born of winning a lottery or a Super Bowl.

Start a journal. (It is not for public consumption, so there's no need to worry about editing your feelings or your grammar.) You can begin by recalling a time, or times, when you felt intoxicated with life. Where were you? At what age? What were the circumstances? And what were the emotions swirling inside you?

Run through a sprinkler with a group of children. If there are no children, run through a sprinkler with a group of senior citizens.

Fill a balloon on a breezy day and let it go. Watch it follow the currents and ride the waves of wind.

Play tag with a butterfly, even if only in your mind.

*Quote for the day:"(Children) get smashed for hours on some strictly limited aspect of the Great Big Everything, the Universe, such as water or snow or mud or colors or rocks" (Kurt Vonnegut ).*

## FOUR

## OBSESSIONS AND DANDELIONS

*Making a garden is not a gentle hobby for the elderly, to be picked up and laid down like a game of solitaire. It is a grand passion. It seizes a person whole, and once it has done so he will have to accept that his life is going to be radically changed. . . .Whatever he had considered to be his profession has become an avocation. His vocation is his garden.*
—May Sarton

My mission on that sunny, late-January morning was straightforward: procure color. Dazzling, make-heads-turn color. Nothing less than stop-'em-dead-in-their-tracks color. This incessant crusade is woven into the fabric of our suburban-bred insecurity. "What will the neighbors think of my front yard now?"

Our local garden center whirred with activity.

The heat of the day had not yet chased the morning dew. Near the entrance, perky wax begonias and chipper winter pansies clustered as an all too cheerful welcoming committee. In stark contrast, and not far from the riotous bloom, were nondescript stacks of black plastic bundles. Each bundle was the size of a narrow football, with two or three heavily waxed green canes protruding from one end. I stood staring at the rows and rows of bare-root roses. On the face of each package glowed a color photo of a flower or flowers in bloom, unsullied and polished. Whatever else I had come for could wait.

On this ordinary January morning, my affair began. I succumbed to a condition for which there is no known cure. Hopelessly smitten, I had to have a rose for my very own.

I returned home from the garden center with thirteen bare-root roses, all hybrid teas or floribundas, picked solely based upon the picture or the allure of the name ('Honor,' 'Mr. Lincoln,' 'Peace,' 'Double Delight'). It's an ingrained American habit, this choosing plants solely from a picture of its flower, as if a bloom is a plant's only function.

As I knew nothing about soil preparation, the new shrubs were put directly into our California clay chalk. Oh, they survived. It takes some doing to kill a rose. And they produced enough blooms to keep our house bright with cut flowers nine or ten months out of the year. As I had nothing to compare to my new paramour, I remained faithful and doting.

I was, after all, a rose gardener. Emphasis on *rose*. That is all that mattered. All other plants in our landscape were a support cast to these divas. There is no middle ground, no halfway, for a rose lover. The desire to obtain, grow, and care for a rose is all-consuming. We are blinded by our adoration. We know nothing, we see nothing but the beloved. For we are an impressionable and fevered lot.

Obsessions do not sprout up unprompted. They grow from a soil that has been worked for years. My free fall began, oddly enough, with my fastidious childhood avoidance of plants. Gardens of any kind, for that matter. Drudgery, after all, is hardly a preferred childhood enterprise.

Flowers in most Midwestern country gardens were a hodge-podge at best, grown for seasonal color, used to liven up the drive-way or front porch flower boxes, or for exhibition at the annual county fair, where 4-H was our way of life. Zinnias, marigolds, asters, and dahlias in garish colors, upright and resolute in their clear vases, several draped in blue ribbons, were exhibited next to barns thick with the smells of apples, cloves, and cinnamon, full of home-baked pies, quilts, and pumpkins the size of Rhode Island.

Walking through these areas, always as a shortcut to the game booths on the midway, it was hard to ignore the evidence that the "garden barns" were the domain of women. Livestock and wood-working were reserved for men. Unfortunately, I had not yet learned to appreciate cows or pigs (as it could be easily argued that they, in turn, cared little for me), and I felt genetically short-changed in the realm of woodworking skills. This social limbo—couldn't milk a cow and I wouldn't be caught dead displaying zinnias in a lace fern bouquet—left me without a peer group, a very tricky place to be in rural America.

As a solution, I hid in my books, living and reliving the eclectic exploits of Robert Louis Stevenson, Zane Grey, and the apostle Paul. Some days I would sit on the living room couch, staring at our floor-to-ceiling bookshelves, crammed with passports to secret worlds where I was free from any need to impress or capitulate. I lived in that dreamworld and saw little need to concern myself with the affairs of this one. Besides, I knew someday that I would score big for God and took solace in the obvious superiority of my calling. Even at this young age, I learned an eagerness for the applause of a rapt congregation.

Dreams or not, every May Day, our mother would send us out into our yard where we grudgingly gathered as many blooms as we could find, from which we would make May Day baskets (fashioned from crepe paper and paste), each dutifully delivered to our neighbors' doors. We would leave the gift on the doorstep or hanging from the doorknob, ring the doorbell, and run. The scent of lilac still brings that memory back, complete with the rejuvenating warmth of the May sun. I picture daffodils, tulips, hyacinths, and cherry blossoms all crammed into those home-made paper containers, and recall my vows that I would never continue such a silly tradition when I got to be in charge.

At the back of our property stood a dozen mature pine trees. Each reached eighty to one hundred feet. One day, I climbed to the top of the tallest, its branches the perfect rungs of a ladder. Less than six feet from the tip, I surveyed my kingdom. I wondered where I would live and make my mark in this world when I left this place, and whether I could see it from my perch. It was spring and the leaves were just breaking on the deciduous trees. The southern Michigan landscape is flat, interrupted by clumps of trees and mirrored lakes. To the south was Long Lake, a playground of my youth. To the west, Mr. Bontrager's corn fields were then a sea of lime green shoots. And to the east stood a marsh.

Probably less than one-half acre in size, the marsh was bigger than a rain forest and imbued with mystery and intrigue for a curious boy. A wetland of garter snakes, muskrats, and bullfrogs. Full of trees and shrubs. There were days when I would ride my bike by, peering into the edges, listening for the baritone rumbling of summer's chorus. And yet, I concluded at that early age, it was delight for children only. It is a fine heritage, to be raised so far removed from concrete and clamor. Even so, when I left home for college at age seventeen, never planning to look back, I was not, nor had I any plans to be, a gardener.

As a young adult, I became easily preoccupied with making my foreordained mark. I set out to be the preacher boy who made good, following the script laid out for my life, climbing that celebrated (but apparently unending) ladder to success. The goal was to "be somebody," and winning the game was fueled in part, no doubt, by a need to distance myself from my rural past, with its parochial worldview, dull pace, and pedestrian predictability. I sought detachment from my past and any weight that might slow me down or prevent my achievement. My new pursuit? A calling commingled with that quintessential American life, built on the unquestioned cornerstones of appearance and image: How do I look? and Who's noticing? I was, after all, a caretaker in God's garden. How much bigger can you get?

My wife and I lived in a nice house, in a nice suburb, where I learned that *nice* doesn't necessarily mean "good for you." Each house in our neighborhood boasted a front yard (*yard,* of course, a word used most liberally in California real estate, implying a space of maybe 400 square feet), which became an implicit membership card to the community. Landowners indeed. As such, your lawn and landscaping, like your life achievements, were the way you were perceived, appraised, and judged. You were obligated to maintain the "correct image." This trust and responsibility was policed by a committee of obsequious and zealous volunteers from the housing association, whose duty it was to keep any creativity at bay, citing each and every violation of the neighborhood appearance code. And there were many potential violations—dull paint, paint not appropriate to the neighborhood color scheme (no shades of mauve or vermilion to be found), brown patches in the yard (earth tones permitted for house color, but not for lawns), or any outlandish (meaning artistically inspired) plant schemes. The incessant insecurity of front-yard upkeep, comparing myself to the neighbors, whose bird of paradise plants are relentlessly in opulent bloom, their suspicious lawn ever so neatly cropped and perennially free of dandelions, became symbolic of my own internal woes.

Our side patch, an enclosed L-shaped courtyard of some 250 square feet, divulged a different story. The stubby end of the L, a brick patio, was roofed with a trellis, under which clay pots of schefflera, ficus, and spathiphyllum thrived, while the elongated segment had just enough room for plantings on either side of a brick walkway. Azalea, agapanthus, and calla lily were flanked by ficus trees. To this mixture I added my newfound hybrid tea roses.

My planting choices were random and haphazard, whatever struck my fancy at the local nursery or flea market. No matter. This courtyard became a sanctuary for me, a safety zone, a place to fuss and futz and not care who was noticing. For being a hero in the church world, or any world, for that matter, is not all that it is cracked up to be. Sooner or later, an escape or solace of any kind becomes inevitable.

It struck me one day that this was the same air I had breathed hanging from the top of that Michigan pine tree as a boy. Or, had I been paying close attention, the same life-giving oxygen I absorbed when I spent an occasional Saturday afternoon roaming the botanical acreage at Huntington Gardens (during my years in graduate school at Pasadena, California). It all marked the beginning, for there was, unbeknownst to me, a conversion afoot.

As a lovelorn and impressionable gardening novice, my rose palate was limited to hybrid tea roses and floribundas. Regardless of any good intentions to the contrary, my style of gardening mirrored my personality, fastidious and suffocating. At the first sight of black spot, that unsightly tobacco-stained leaf tattoo, I would dash to the garden center for advice and a chemical cure-all. Whatever would do the trick.

Armed like an engineer at a nuclear waste site, I waded through the rose beds, spraying, coating, doing battle, and kicking butt. All very Ramboesque. Outfitted with sprayer and powder, I drenched the leaves, daring the disease to challenge me. I sprayed, therefore I was a rose gardener.

Sooner or later, it dawns on you that, like buying a pet, you can't begin to anticipate the endless list of requisite supplemental products. Each trip to the garden center extended my slate of dictated accessories, giving one the clue that as a gardener it would be easier just to stick dollar bills directly into the soil. Even so, I acquired fertilizer (both granular and powder), insecticide, fungicide, dolomite lime, face masks, gloves, loppers, and spray nozzles for an exterminator. I purchased them all with abandon, no questions asked. And certainly no concern for the greater issues of toxic chemicals or poisons or any adverse affect on my environment. For thoroughly mixed into, and radically coloring, this mosaic was my religious heritage: Fundamentalist Protestant. "This world is not my home, we're just a passin' through," we sang lustily, learning any attachments to the old terra firma were ill-advised at best and more than likely a barrier to our relationship with God. This contradiction—worshiping a God who created so lush and fruitful a creation set against the notion that it was all so similar to a Styrofoam cup, somehow easily discarded when used—was never questioned. Beauty, if anything, was simply appreciation for the pragmatic and the blemish-free.

Without question, I wished for my first love to be pristine. There could be no doubt that my zeal flamed eager and impassioned, if only a tad misplaced. In time, you come to suspect this unswerving devotion and chalk it up to some kind of vitamin deficiency, hoping that fate will grant you a more docile and manageable pastime.

Black spot and powdery mildew, of course, are synonymous with roses, and are particularly fond of modern varieties (the kind with which I fell in love). In other words, you don't just buy a hybrid tea rose; you buy a spray and care regimen that requires ongoing vigilance and perseverance. Doting rapidly mutates into the around-the-clock regimen of an intensive care nurse, which is the price we pay in this culture to be blotch- and blemish-free.

My hybrid tea roses became a wonderful metaphor for my image consciousness. Funginex became my horticultural Retin A.

Even so, to my wonderment, my hybrid tea roses bloomed and mesmerized, despite the ongoing chemical warfare on their soil. You want dazzling flowers—I'll give you dazzling flowers. Which meant that I stayed vigilant for any signs of malady or disease.

Hybrid tea roses, I learned with time, turned out to be far more show than substance. But I was young, full of energy, naive, and susceptible to high-maintenance women.

May Sarton warned that gardening is not for the young, because we are too impatient and self-absorbed. And it did not take long for my new garden sanctuary to feel infiltrated by the same uneasiness that drove me there in the first place. I could feel my passion becoming claustrophobic, another way for gauging and measuring, for posturing and preening. Obsessions do not sit well with our need to tinker.

My hunch is that we do it in all of our relationships. Tinker. We fall in love with what makes someone unique. And then we spend the next several years doing our best to change them. Flaws are to be tolerated, and then methodically eliminated. It comes with the package. I wanted a passion and a life sprinkled liberally with that passion. I also wanted my passion to be containable and controllable. You know, passion with the freedom to tinker. We don't want our passion to change us. We want it to change every-one else around us. That's the way it is supposed to be. Or is it?

A man who took great pride in his lawn
found himself with a large crop of dandelions.
He tried every method he knew to get rid of them.
Still they plagued him.
Finally he wrote to the Department of Agriculture.
He enumerated all the things he had tried

and closed his letter with the question,
"What shall I do now?"
In due course the reply came:
"We suggest you learn to love them."
  —Anthony de Mello

Truth is, hybrid tea roses exist as the result of man's quest for the perfect flower. As a species, roses have been around for a few million years. The hybrid tea cultivars are the very new kids on the block, having been in cultivation for only a little over one hundred years. Once the ever blooming roses of China were crossed with the hardy, fragrant, old garden roses of Europe, the race was on to develop a better rose, one with a larger and more frequent bloom and a flawless flower. The culmination of this obsession came in 1867, when 'La France,' the first hybrid tea and precursor to our modern rose, was begot.

In an ironic twist, our obsession shifted from appreciating the plant itself to our need for a perfect plant. It's an insidious demand, this race toward a glasslike bloom. Perfection, of course, is never without its price. One could easily argue that while representing passion gone amok, hybrid tea roses also champion a passion gone sterile. We end up with pristine flowers at the expense of character, and even scent.

Fortunately, there are modern prophets aplenty, waving their arms and hoping we take notice, shouting their warnings whether we listen or not. "Perhaps what really happened in 1867 was a monumental act of horticultural repression," Michael Pollan writes. "For the hybrid roses don't give more bloom, really, they just parcel their blooms out over a longer period; they save to reinvest. So instead of abandoning herself to one great climax of bloom, the rose now doles out her blossoms one by one, always holding back, forever on the verge, never quite . . . finishing. The idea of a flower that never finishes would have struck the Elizabethans as perverse; one of the things they loved most about the rose was the way it held nothing back, the way it bloomed unreservedly and then was spent."

Henry Mitchell is never shy about adding his angle. "There is nothing wrong, . . . or at least nothing utterly evil, in raising scentless roses that require weekly spraying and that can be sheltered and shielded, patted and pampered, until at last an enormous flower can be entered in a rose show. Without rose shows, and without roses that have never been outside an intensive care unit, society would suffer. Many people who are now safely occupied with the care of roses would be loose on the streets."

Stephen Lacey takes a more subtle approach: "[hybrid tea roses] have no personality, no natural manner of growth to enable them to blend gently with their neighbors, and in winter they look hideous."

Indeed.

What a quandary I found myself in. The love of my life, my anemic, chemical-coated hybrid tea roses, began to pale.

At about the same time, my wife and I spent one week at Langford cottage, tucked into a sedate village in the heart of the Cotswolds. A cast-iron gate hung on a golden chestnut stone wall. Spilling over the wall and crowding the gate was *Rosa mundi,* a sprawling Gallica rose bush, canes loaded with blooms lax and nonchalant. Its flowers are white with red swaths liberally painted. Its charm is in its disarming candy-colored innocence. The back wall of the cottage supported 'Rambling Rector,' a thirty foot rambling rose with an explosion of single white blooms.

On the same trip, we visited Kiftsgate, a late-nineteenth-century estate sitting on the northwest edge of the Cotswolds.

The several-acre gardens were originally developed in 1918. Old garden roses lined the walkways. There was 'William Lobb,' a deep crimson-maroon moss rose. And 'Pax,' a six-foot mound of snowy white Hybrid Musk blooms. Above it all flourishes the original Kiftsgate rose, now an imperial mantle, literally draped over the shoulders of a seventy-foot Copper Beech tree.

These are old garden roses. And their variety is legion. From the wiry, lanky canes of the ground cover *Rosa paulii* with its simple large, white single blooms, to the deep quartered and crimson Gallica roses, to the swollen cabbage-sized blooms of the Centifolias.

My infatuation could not be suppressed. Although pangs of guilt began to beat me about the brow. Once again, I wore the shame of the culpable philanderer. My first love wavering, now enamored by a new love.

But then, perhaps I wasn't meant for fidelity, the standard party line went, as I rolled these rationalizations over and over in my mind. After all, I needed a new interest every few years. So it makes sense that I was dumping the fickle younger hybrid tea for an antique rose, the older woman. There can't be any shame in that, can there?

What was utterly refreshing to me was the realization that not all roses are alike, straitjacketed into the prissy elegance of the sterile buds for mass-market sales on Valentine's Day. Not all roses need persistent oversight.

Perhaps it was I who had begun to change. Or is it that my love was evolving? Could it be? To see the rose for what it could give me, without the necessity to keep the dear lady drugged.

Most old garden roses are shrubs commingled with a story, a peculiar history, or perhaps even a legend. *Rosa mundi*, for example, dates to at least 1581. The legend is told that the flower was named after Fair Rosamund, mistress of Henry II, which makes me wonder if that was the benefaction for all his mistresses. To my way of thinking, it beats a diamond necklace.

Not far from my house grows the native *Rosa nutkana,* a plant which grew here 35 million years ago. It's kind of hard to get your mind around numbers that big. Still robust after all these years, *Rosa nutkana* can be a great tangled clump of a plant—a wonderful hedge row, as in you couldn't drive a car through it—sporting a mass of dainty, single pink blooms each spring.

There is no doubt that we are still drawn to the still-life beauty of the hybrid tea bloom—in the same way we assume our bodies should match the well-oiled abs and pecks of those paraded in the ads of glossy magazines. But compared to the prissy and self-conscious youthful arrogance of the hybrid tea, old garden roses carry themselves with the air of self-confidence that ennobles a full-bodied and sensual middle-aged woman. For her power is not in her need to tease.

Rather than ending my affair with the rose, old garden roses have only served to give it new life and let some of the compulsive air escape. This love was no longer about primping, but about respites of soothing and islands of calm. Like the Greeks of Homer's day, I learned to grow roses for their perfume, in order to keep illness at bay—"by day and by night, she washed the skin with rose oil" (*Iliad,* Book XXIII).

I'm the first to admit that my love for old garden roses makes me a snob. Of this there is no doubt. But I am a snob who is still enamored and enthralled by his *Rosa inamorata.*

From a California townhouse, we moved to three woodland acres on an island in Puget Sound, near Seattle, Washington.

Gardening isn't a hobby anymore. It is a lifestyle, a paradigm shift. It is no longer about landscaped color or upgrades in the landscape. Gardening is about seeing. Gardening is about aware-ness. Gardening is the antithesis of the tyranny that comes from some imaginary competition with the neighborhood, a percep-tion that you are being judged by how your lawn is mowed.

It is autumn. Fourteen years and fifteen hundred miles sepa-rate me from that novice, the one seen kneeling and fussing over plants on that suburban patio. I just walked in from my morning jaunt with our two dogs and am wandering through the back gar-den. Some moles were busy last night, fortuitously eluding our cats, while leaving their telltale piles of evidence. The leaves of the katsura tree hang limp and pale yellow. In a breeze, they shimmer as a wind chime. I stop at the Bourbon rose, 'Madame Isaac Pereire,' still with a handful of blooms in mid-October, and bury my nose in a blossom, its heady sweet fragrance a bracing effect no less potent than Seattle espresso. The buds are tight and cov-ered with dew. New lateral growth shines with a deep merlot red contrast. Rose hips hang like unpicked crab apples suspended from the *Rosa rugosa* canes nearby. And I smile, ear to ear, that trademark giddy and whimsical grin associated with folks not quite all there. It just cannot be helped.

I stop to sit on our front deck. My mind goes back nine years, to my first trip to our new Northwest island home. My wife and I had decided to leave the Los Angeles area, choosing to settle in the Pacific Northwest, hoping to find a gentler, less hectic space. I presumed that moving was the answer, hoping, unrealistically, to outrun whatever may have plagued me. At the time, I didn't real-ize the important role the land would play.

It was a warm September day when we arrived. I sprawled on my back, on the grass already bronzed from the summer heat. The sky above me had edges, and looked moored by the jutting fir and cedar trees around our lot. I heard bees, and beyond them, silence. Outside of the cities, you are framed by the stillness. It becomes your reference point. Not far from me, a plum tree spread its copious and gnarled branches. The earth beneath me felt solid. My lungs filled. As I lay there, I breathed in something intangible, and although I couldn't name it, I knew I was starting to reclaim something I had lost long ago.

Not long after, I found myself catapulting down the Colorado River toward my fated rendezvous with an iris.

Today, old garden roses litter the half-acre garden tucked around our island home, all reminders of what it means to be seized whole. From the unique *Sericea pteracantha,* with its large talon-like, translucent crimson thorns. To the backdrop hedge of *Rosa moyesii,* loaded with hips through the autumn and winter. To the delicate pink flowers of the groundcover rose 'Nozomi.' To the luxuriant fragrance of the Bourbon rose 'Lauriel de Barney.' *Rosa rugosa,* 'La Reine Victoria,' 'Sally Holmes,' 'Chapeau de Napoleon,' and the Bourbon 'Souvenir de la Malmaison.' And yes, there are even a few hybrid tea roses. There's no need to be a complete purist just to prove a point. Is there?

One big difference. I've retired my spray paraphernalia and chemical regimen (what a garage sale). Black spot and powdery mildew still rear their nettlesome heads. So be it. I'm learning to accept that this garden is for plants and peace, not warfare and worry.

Anthony de Mello continues:

I too had a lawn I prided myself in.
Filled with dandelions which I fought
with every means of my power.

So learning to love them was no easy matter.
I began by talking to them each day,
you know, cordial, friendly like.
But they maintained a sullen silence.
They were still smarting from the war
I had waged against them,
and they were suspicious of my motives.
But I continued. And it wasn't long before they smiled back.
And soon we became friends.
My lawn, of course, was ruined.
But how beautiful my new garden became.

# SOUL GARDENING EXERCISES

## Obsessions and Dandelions

Make a May Day basket, regardless of the month. (Pick one day each month to be May Day.) Fill the basket—crepe paper or construction paper or wrapping paper lined with plastic—with whatever may be in season: cherry blossoms, pansies, tulips, fern fronds, Queen Anne's lace. Hang it anonymously on someone's door, or place it on someone's desk.

Buy a large clay pot and plant a dandelion garden. (Go into your local nursery and ask for dandelion seeds—just to see the look on the clerk's face.)

Better yet, if you have any dandelions in your lawn, let them bloom (okay, in at least one corner of your lawn).

Spend an afternoon at a local park watching children play. Notice what it is like to be seized whole by an endeavor or activity.

What is it that seizes you whole? What is it that captures your heart, your passion?

*Quote for the day:"Happy is the man . . . his delight is in the law of the Lord, and on his law he meditates day and night. He is like a tree planted by streams of water, that yields its fruit in its season, and its leaf does not wither"(Psalms 1:1-3, New English Bible).*

# AUTUMN

*To be free to hear the music, instead
of worrying about the right notes . . .
To embrace the demanding marriage
of loving and losing*

# A RECIPE IS NOT A HANDCUFF

*We live life like ill-taught piano students . . .*
*so inculcated with the flub that gets us in dutch,*
*we don't hear the music, we only play the right notes.*
—Robert Capon

Yesterday delivered an uncharacteristically saturated July day. The backdrop felt like November, sullied by unrelenting showers, dogged drizzle, and medieval mist. It was a Saturday for reshuffling plans. A day more suited to napping, sipping coffee, and catching up on back issues of the *New Yorker*.

Today, however, the sun reemerges and the sky fills a somewhat hopeful blue, flecked with ivory clouds, random and placid. First on the agenda: assess yesterday's damage. Regardless of the benefit, a full day of stormy rain takes its toll on a perennial garden—any garden, for that matter—and first impressions always give more worry than is warranted. I am a caricature, pacing like an overanxious father, regarding any threat to my sheltered children as a declaration of war. The roses, with blooms weighted by water, are bowed, limbs sprawled to the ground like abject penitents awaiting absolution. The plum tree mimics the shape of a grand canopy, swollen and closer to the ground. The spiked perennials (delphinium, thalictrum, and foxglove) didn't fare so well. Most plants bent to the breaking point, irreparable, fated to a spasmodic and flimsy posture, with limbs as obdurate as those of the scarecrow in the *Wizard of Oz*.

One theory, of course, is to let 'em bend. Let nature have its way. This is a good theory on a sunny day, but not necessarily today, as I wander around the beds lamenting and cursing and repairing, as if the plants are dependent upon my fastidious attention. Which, of course, is true if one is trying to maintain some type of image, demanding that every rose bush stand full, symmetrical, and impervious to nature's inconveniences—every plant in its assigned place, every stalk erect, primping for some glossy effigy.

My immediate portentous wail, fists raised to the sky, fills the air, "Let it be known that I shall quit gardening altogether and move to the Caribbean." Then I yell, at whomever, for whatever good measure, "Who needs it?" And, as always, the sky is silent. There is no reply. So, I take the only obvious course of action. I decide to sit and stew. I sit on the deck and talk to my dog. After an hour or so, we come to some consensus and decide not to sweat it, what with the delphinium stalks lain askew over the way- ward branches of the rose 'Trier' and the Miscanthus grass doing its best Tower of Pizza. As the quirkiness grows on you, the remaining residual need for unyielding control is whittled away, at least for today. Ever so slowly, one digests that gardens, like mir- acles, cannot be regulated. Or controlled.

We're big on control in this culture. All things in their proper places. And we don't want anything to be askew, now, do we?

I'm not sure where this notion originated. Is it genetic or in our drinking water? Not that pinpointing the origin matters. But there is no arguing that the premise is endemic to our world— namely, that our success, our very value, is measured by our capacity for playing the right notes.

We bend over backward to explain or defend whatever may appear to be a weakness, a chink in our armor. And if there is a chink, we exercise damage control, with justifications all around. My own garden tours for friends and guests are sprinkled with explication, "That area's not meant to be that way. We plan on making some changes."

"Oh that. Well, that's not finished yet."

"Yes, we're going to tear that out and . . . zippity do da, zippity ay" (as if the clarification somehow bolsters public opinion and assures the listener that you are not nearly on the edge). Which begs the question, on the edge of what? Are we to fear Mr. Blackwell lurking in the shrubbery, leading some natty garden patrol?

Our exterior is only an inevitable reflection of what goes on inside. I once had a conversation with a woman who was telling me some of her life story. Like any such story, we came upon one of the inevitable sad pockets. Unfeigned tears brimmed above both cheeks.

"I'm sorry," she apologized quickly.

I said, "Excuse me?" assuming I had missed something.

"I'm sorry for crying," she blurted, the back of her hand rubbing away the spillage. "I shouldn't cry."

Heaven forbid. As if every emotion comes with some moral red flag, and we are required to put on the right face for the right people, buying into the belief that certain emotions are incorrect, somehow taboo and shameful.

While this is not about emotions, they make a good indicator plant (those plants that tell us what we can expect to grow in certain soils), and our need to keep them in check provides adequate confirmation of our craving for correct appearances.

As a consequence, we pride ourselves on being in control. It is, after all, un-American to be out of control. Some would argue the matter, no doubt. They would point out that we Americans are the epitome of a nation "out of control." Reckless, maybe. Without boundaries, for certain. But not without a compulsion for order. Even our rage is stylized. So we set about the task of putting life's categories into boxes. Neatly arranged. Predictable. No surprises. We enjoy those times when we believe our emotions are in check, and we can carry an acceptable and adult demeanor.

When I fessed up to being an adult child of an alcoholic, I raced to the nearest bookstore to buy ten books on adult children of alcoholics, reading most of them that first weekend. It was simple. I was going to heal, or recover, faster than anyone in the history of this disease. These inclinations were fostered from the time I went through a divorce convinced that I had apparently not been grieving correctly, as if *my* process was homework about to be returned with a red checkmark, requiring that I go back to the beginning of the grief cycle or, at the very least, stay after school and write on the chalkboard one hundred times, "I'm sorry, I shouldn't feel this way."

There's a story about a woman with a serious case of hives who went to a specialist for relief. She had suffered much, living for some time in continual pain, because the hives covered most of her body. She needed healing, and hoped that the doctor could prescribe a cure. But his diagnosis surprised her. "There's no physical reason for your hives," he told her, and then paused. "So, it's my conclusion that your skin is crying because you cannot."

And so it is with us. We all pay the price from emotions, or lives, held in check. Not completely sure how to identify them, or what to do with them once they're in the light, we keep most of our feelings buried under layers of good intentions, mostly due to our suspicion about their power, or our fear of losing our cool, or the lingering attention paid to our manicured reputations. In her book *New Passages,* Gail Sheehy talks about actress Lauren Hutton's struggle. "All anybody had paid and praised her for all through her first adulthood was her outer appearance, her false self. 'I'd been striking stances, and imitations of stances, all my professional life,' she says. 'They were getting further and further away from the truth of how I felt.'"

Ain't it so? Our emotions seem to be party crashers, which, like the little brother who tags along on big sister's date, are always uninvited and bothersome. So we work hard at keeping an appropriate front, practicing life management—which is that finely tuned skill of keeping emotions contained. "What will they think?" we ask frequently and rhetorically, never completely determining who *they* are anyway.

Of course, the consequence is a boatload of hours spent tidying up the emotional landscape of our front yard, just in case anybody happens to drive by.

I have a friend who wants a fairway for a lawn. You know: lush, flourishing, inviting, carpetlike, surreal. His problem: it's a fair-sized lawn (sixty by ninety feet) and fully colonized by dandelions. Like most of us, he was weaned on the axiom that it is appearance we're paid and praised for, by which standard his present lawn is an embarrassment. In his mind, there is no alternative. He wants to kill it—the entire lawn—and start over. But I can't give him too much grief. I've been in those shoes.

It is the way I gardened for years. You see, perennial is somewhat of an anomaly in Southern California, since many annuals—impatiens, begonias, petunias, ubiquitous vinca *(Catharanthus roseus)*, and salvia (both the blue *farinacea* and the garish red *splendens)*—are grown for year-round color, preferably in riotous bloom. Downtime, winter dormancy, fallow season are all kept at bay, like some stifling morality to be avoided.

I easily fell into the hypervigilance trap. When any of my flowers looked a little ragged, I yanked them, chucked them into a trash container, marched off to the local nursery, flashed my charge card, and loaded the trunk of my car with fresh color. It is the modern suburban way, after all: disposable gardens. It is ingrained—

seasonal change and foliage are secondary to color splash and bloom. (And devotees of the disposable know that green, of course, unless it is a lush lawn, is not considered a color.)

I do agree with Michael Pollan's assessment that "suburban America has been laid out to look best from the perspective not of its inhabitants, but of the motorist." So this is our heritage: gardening based upon public opinion. And we are reduced to garden management.

So be it. If those were the rules, I could excel right along with the best of them. I consulted catalogs and garden masters. Books littered my desk, recommending and advocating specific designs with surefire plants. The temptation here is instant gratification. We are bewitched by pictures and graphics of completed borders stuffed with ornamentals specifically chosen to perform and delight, all delivered in a planting guide resembling a paint-by-number canvas.

I remember that novice, on hands and knees, tape measure in hand, meting out recommended plant spacing with exasperating precision. The plants, meager and inadequate, looked forlorn. But then, for heaven's sake, he didn't want to do it wrong—continuing to glance at the catalog picture after each plant went into the ground, just to make sure he figured correctly. "Don't screw up, don't screw up," was his unswerving mantra.

There is no doubt I was a whole-hog convert. Both feet. In the deep end. That my ideas and dreams were several steps ahead of my pocketbook and time goes without saying, and many wonderful projects had to wait. Although in gardening, "We'll build it next year" is a difficult sentence to speak or swallow.

So be it. I kept a fretful eye on the vigilant watchman in me, waiting to see how I would be judged.

I remember walking my one-year-old Seattle garden, a time for appraisal and discovery, to see how my dreams had translated from paper to soil. I saw some of what I had expected. In bloom, poppies are exotic and charming. But when they're done blooming, their foliage looks like the aftermath of a Fourth of July parade. Other sights startled me. The recommended vinca minor is now a raging Pandora, burying lesser plants and lawn chairs in its wake. Most of my lupine was crippled by slugs (our cool wet Junes are a Club Med for the heartless beasts), who had nibbled sizable chunks from the stalks, causing the plants to wilt, droop, and do a good imitation of a compost heap in the middle of the border. There's not much to do but curse and mutter, waving the white flag to the obstinate monster, letting them know the battle was theirs. But the war, most assuredly, goes on. Yet, what to do with the unsightly gaps where lupines should still be blooming? And what of the other plants, the ones that, for no apparent reason, just flat out died?

It's then, if you're lucky, while muttering and repairing, that the garden's surprises will rattle your persnickety cage. Surprises, the garden's very music, always seem to infiltrate from outside the realm of our careful plans and exacting preparation. Like the rose that had been given up for dead, proudly displaying one single bloom. It's color light lavender, scented with lemons (another wonderful surprise). Or near the plum tree, where a patch sprinkled with bluebells *(Scilla)* emerged as if by magic, a springtime nodding carpet of indigo. Or off the back fence, where a thicket of elderberry shows off its red fruits, advertising an avian Sunday buffet. Or the ambushing spiced pungency from the indistinct winter blooms of the evergreen shrub *Sarcococca,* conjuring memories of Grandmother's kitchen and hugs that don't quit. Or the back-path congregation of bunchberry springing as diminutive vigil lights with spirited white flames. Or the mistake, that mystery plant I bought—from the nursery that isn't always careful with its marker tabs—which turned out to be a *Campanula lactiflora,* purple bellflowers pointing skyward on several breezy medium-height stalks.

So, you stop what you are doing and watch the clouds roll through the northern sky, a current of billowy statuary. The wind is out of the southwest, filling your lungs and restoring something that had been missing, and you catch a glimpse of two rufous hummingbirds providing an acrobatic air show for no one in particular.

Image consciousness and gardening don't mix.

Image consciousness and any enterprise where the soul is involved don't mix. But isn't that the beginning of understanding spirituality? To be image conscious keeps our guard up. It keeps our judgments—about ourselves, others, and God—sharply defined, for we want to make sure we play the right notes. Thus, we are unable to hear the music, which is another way of saying we are unable to receive, to welcome, to embrace. Or, to pray.

In his book *Dark Intimacy,* David Hassel explains it this way:

> In prayer of being, I am tempted to let God be God. This means that I do not try to imprison God inside my present conception or image of him. I may even let God break my idol-images of him, no matter how elaborate the conception, no matter how comfortable I am with a particular image and how uncomfortable with some new image crafted by traumatic events.

This all means that when we're back in the garden, we give ourselves the permission to hear the music by looking beneath the garden's physical dimension. The garden's exterior, its development, I can easily explain. I can take you on a tour and show you around. I can calmly illuminate the reasons behind the design: why we used weathered granite to form walls here, and raised beds and pavers for the walkway there, why conifers are appropriate for that corner, and so on.

But that doesn't quite explain the garden, which is spiritual at its core, a mystical place of solace and surprises and secrets, a place where we can wander and wonder and generally lose ourselves. This morning a gauze of fog has spilled into the canyon. Dew hangs from the remaining leaves of the big-leaf maple. The lingering blooms of the bourbon rose 'Louise Odier,' a deep pink in the winter light, serve as the brace for an elaborate spider-webbed necklace, bejeweled with strings of water crystals.

An hour or so outside of Seattle, you can find yourself on a trail in an old-growth forest with trees older than George Washington, only a stone's throw from the interstate. The sound of your footsteps is swallowed by the sponged carpet—thousands of years of composted leaves, branches, trees, and critters. It is rarer than gold, this humus so dark and rich. A river spills over glacial rock, each massive stone placed with precision some 15,000 years prior by an anonymous landscaper. You stop, look up, hear the music, and feel your spirit soar.

Needless to say, we're confronted with a paradigm shift here. It has to do not so much with gardening, but with the audience.

There is a great scene in the musical *A Chorus Line* where the director asks one of the auditioners, "Who are you dancing for?" Whose opinion really matters here anyway?

Precisely.

No doubt we've all been inculcated into the realities and nuances of dysfunctional families and their mark on us all. It is our cultural legacy. When I was in college, meeting someone was straightforward, "What's your sign?" Now, you walk up to a total stranger and ask, "What's your dysfunction?" Unfortunately, they answer you.

The basic and undeniable premise is that we all bring with us baggage from our family systems, hoping, with that baggage, to compensate for whatever we may have lacked. So sort through the baggage we do, now that we understand the rules. It is an industry, this exploration, and there are many who would add fuel to the fire with a pep talk about how enough willpower and self-control can get you out from under the weight. You can become forever slender, ever confident, and codependent no more!

I'm a big fan of Sally, Charlie Brown's little sister. She went to summer camp and was supposed to have been gone an entire week. But she returned home the day after she went. Charlie Brown asked, "I thought you were at camp?" "I was," Sally replied. "They said if I went to camp, it would be good for me. They said if I went to camp, I would find myself. Well, I got off the bus, and there I was. So I came home."

One can only wonder why having our act together is the unrelenting ambition, especially given the added weight of shame for the one who perpetually falls short. "Lord have mercy," as my grandfather would mutter. Perhaps it's not such a bad idea to sport a Tee-shirt that shouts, "codependent still, but still okay," believing that inside all of us there's a kernel of dignity and value, and we can hold our heads high even if we didn't ace the test. Surely we are not defined by whether or not we have "recovered," are we?

However you slice it, getting your act together (or playing the right notes) is not a good compulsion to take with you into the garden. It may feel natural when you begin your day, but by afternoon the weight is awkward and an all-round nuisance. Not to mention that it's more invasive and harder to eradicate than morning glory. And the whole load messes with your head at the most inopportune moments. Sitting on the garden deck, you notice an empty space in one of the beds. You become as manic as a middle-aged man with a bald spot. All of life is put on hold until that glaring incrimination is rectified. By that time your beer is warm, or your coffee is cold. Either way you look at it, you're standing befuddled on the garden path, forgetting why the chair on the deck beckoned you in the first place.

Like many who garden, I love to cook. The stages of learning are predictable. First, you spend hours wandering about the kitchen, unable to identify major appliances. But slowly you learn. You try recipes, simple ones, glancing several times to make sure you have complied with the instructions to the precise milliliter. And then one day, quite by accident, you realize that the recipe is not a handcuff, but a suggestion. An idea for a mingling of flavor. And as you are tasting a sauce, it occurs to you that a pinch of basil or oregano would just do the trick. It is then that you realize, you are a cook. No Julia Child, to be sure. But why is that the only option?

It is no different in the garden. As novices, we too easily rely on experts (who are often just celebrities with a hand trowel) to tell us how to live, and garden, by buying the right tools, wearing the right clothes, planting the right plant. Sure, it's great to get advice, and fascinating to hear what others suggest—what they plant and why. But not at the expense of being afraid to risk. Or afraid to trust our instincts. Which leaves us so fearful of being wrong.

There's a terrific story about a first-grade Sunday school class. The children were restless and fussy. The teacher, in an attempt to get their attention, said, "Okay kids, let's play a game. I'll describe something to you. And you tell me what it is."

The kids quieted down.

"Listen. It's a furry little animal with a big bushy tail, that climbs up trees and stores nuts in the winter. Who can tell me what it is?"

No one said anything.

The teacher went on. "You are a good Sunday school class. You know the right answer to this question. It's a furry little animal with a big bushy tail, that climbs up trees and stores nuts in the winter."

One little girl raised her hand.

"Emily?"

"Well, teacher," Emily declared, "it sounds like a squirrel to me, but I'll say Jesus."

We start young in this culture. Scared to death to be wrong.

No one is born a gardener. Much as we'd like to think that skill and predisposition cards were handed out in the heavens, and that some people won the genetic lottery in the green thumb department. There is no doubt that some have perfected the touch. We stand before their masterpieces and ogle and envy and shake our heads in disbelief. Too often, the intimidation sets us back, squelching any motivation we had to start our own garden, and we resort to taking pictures on our vacations. Or, if we have enough money, we can hire a pro to come in and gussy up the place for us. It is no different with other parts of our lives—those times we live vicariously through someone else who appears to have their ducks in a row.

For those of us who've mustered the courage to give a garden a whirl, we have lived through those days when the slugs sponsored conventions on our delphiniums and hostas, or the deer sent thank-you notes for our thoughtfulness in planting so many delicacies, or the squirrels and moles decided to have a treasure hunt for most of the tulip bulbs we planted last fall, or the rain left our perennials disheveled as a hangover. We've been there. And we wonder what sort of supplication is necessary to inspire some garden god to rally to our cause.

We stand outside our house, surveying the lot and taking mental inventory, when it occurs to us that this is it: this street, this house, these trees, that woman or man or child. *This is my life.*

The rich industrialist from the North was horrified to find the southern fisherman lying lazily beside his boat, smoking a pipe.

"Why aren't you out fishing?" the industrialist asked.

"Because I have caught enough fish for the day," said the fisherman.

"Why don't you catch some more?"

"What would I do with them?"

"You could earn more money," was the reply. "With that you could have a motor fixed to your boat and go into deeper waters and catch more fish. Then you would make enough to buy nylon nets. These would bring you more fish and more money. Soon you would have enough money to own two boats, maybe even a fleet of boats. Then you would be a rich man like me."

"What would I do then?" asked the fisherman.

"Then you could really enjoy life."

"What do you think I'm doing right now?"

Gardening is about being grounded, rooted to the here and now without the need to tidy up. It is the difference between managing life and entering into life, reminding us that gardening need not be the fraught, perfectionistic, slightly paranoid struggle that it becomes for some. Truth is, our love of plants is bound up with a taste for human error, nature's excesses, and sheer unadulterated indulgence.

My two buddies, Arnold Lobel's Frog and Toad, talk about a garden. Frog gives Toad some seeds to plant, which he does. But

Toad is overanxious, wanting his garden to grow quickly. Frog reassures him it will.

"But how soon?" Toad demands. And he tries everything: reading poems to his seeds, singing songs to his seeds, lighting candles for his seeds at night, fearing that they may be afraid of the dark.

Nothing.

Finally, Frog gives him some advice, "Leave them alone for a few days. Let the sun shine on them, let the rain fall on them. Soon your seeds will start to grow."

And, of course, while Toad was taking a nap, they did just that.

Frog was right, you know. Gardening can be an extension of my posturing. Life lived to be noticed or liked, or right. So let's set the record straight. Life is not a contest.

Or a race.

Or a beauty pageant.

And God isn't some game show host ready to reward your correct answers with a Buick in the clouds. Although, wouldn't you know it, that Buick happens to be your favorite color.

The summer squall aftermath is still in evidence. I'm not sure if I'll get around to cleanup today. Maybe next week. Certainly before visitors see the unsightly mess. Indeed.

In the meanwhile, my dog and I pick up our conversation where we left off, and a breeze ripples the spent blooms of Oceanspray, now a shrub of six-foot wands waving unpretentious rusted lanterns. The sun peeks around a giant cottonwood, creating dark geometric pools throughout the garden. Two butterflies claim squatters' rights on a splayed and broken delphinium. Apparently there is no need to tell them I meant to clean all that up.

# SOUL GARDENING EXERCISES

## A Recipe Is Not a Handcuff

What is there about our emotions that requires a moral price tag? Do you find yourself inadvertently assigning such tags to your own emotions? In what way does it benefit or hinder?

Keep a journal for a month, making entries about your emotional life. This is not to record merely what we are feeling, but how we view those emotions, and why we categorize certain emotions as good or bad.

Read the stories about Jesus' life in the Gospels (try Luke, chapters 7–9 and Mark, chapter 10). They are stories about interruptions—by curious children, persistent senior citizens, and image-conscious rich folk. Yet, Jesus never seems out of sorts—somehow embracing the interruptions as a part of life.

What is it that bothers us about interruption in this culture? What is being interrupted? What are we afraid of losing?

Where does contentment actually come from? What do the advertisers promise? What are they really attempting to sell us?

Reread the parable of the fisherman and the rich industrialist (page 102). Can you recall a time when you experienced the fisherman's contentment, the industrialist's myopic quest for success? What were the ingredients? The circumstances?

Practice belly laughter. Seated comfortably, hold your belly with both hands, and laugh until your body shakes. Or get a group of friends and try it as a group activity.

*Quote for the day:"Enlightenment is just another word for feeling comfortable with being a completely ordinary person"(Veronique Vienne).*

# SIX

## MAGNIFICENT HEARTBREAKS

*Is childhood ever long enough, or a happy time, or even a*
*beautiful summer day? All of these carry the seeds*
*of the same fierce mystery that we call death.*
——Eugene Kennedy

*Wherever humans garden magnificently,*
*there are magnificent heartbreaks.*
——Henry Mitchell

Some years back, early after my move to the Pacific Northwest, I spent each spring morning surveying my newly created garden kingdom. This realm boasted, among other things, my first official "rose garden." Showcased in an area thirty by twenty feet, surrounded by a tidy and formal clipped boxwood hedge, it carried the aura of an official tea garden. Every morning I wandered the property, incessantly returning to the rose bed, inspecting and perusing, delighted that the young shrubs were robust, their new shoots a burgundy red, each bush proudly displaying vestal buds. What could I say? All was right with the world. And each day I charged into the garden wishing for a miracle, hoping to catch a bud in that twinkling act of unfurling. But miracles are never without a price.

One morning I stopped, immobilized at the boxwood hedge. Most of the young rose plants looked fully shorn, like unwitting victims of an overnight military haircut. Vestal buds, new shoots, burgundy leaves, and composure—all gone.

Unnerved, I knelt, gently touching the hurt. I had no preparation for this. And I wasn't sure why. Except that it is not masculine to be undone by the death of a flower. Regardless, the remainder of the morning played out as a full-blown Irish wake, and I meandered, wailing and moaning, a cursing banshee.

There is something rudimentarily disorienting about disarray and the loss it represents. It calls into question our very sense of wellbeing. Tragedy, of any scope, is not—it cannot be—in the script. At least not the one we were handed by our well-meaning parents who did their best to protect us from tooth decay, godless communists, and any other trespass on our happiness.

Pain-free is our national birthright, an entitlement. One fed by compelling images from ubiquitous Prozac ads to the landscaping at Disney world, with its gussied islands of strategic clusters where masses of bedding plants, marigolds, petunias, and their ilk create smiling cartoon faces with nary a weed to be found. It is colorful, tidy, precise, and antiseptic—and in its own way, doggone it all, quite charming. We live in a culture where tidiness can be terribly reassuring.

I've been there, consumed by the expectation—no, the demand—that there be no leaf out of place. And yes, I even expected the weather to cooperate. Perhaps it's connected to my need to subdue. Or so my convoluted logic goes. If I can control, then certainly, I am not at the mercy of. Or maybe it's all connected to the same gland that soothes and sedates, like warm milk and cookies at bedtime.

So anyway, I'm standing at the edge of my rose garden, my world on tilt and the Rolling Stones's "You Can't Always Get What You Want" coursing through my head, which is a great song until you realize that it's about your own life. Even so, after a day of sulking, I decided to get on with my life, play sleuth and get to the bottom of the mystery.

What mean-spirited creature could do such a thing to my roses?

It didn't take long to find the answer. The next morning between 6:30 and 7:00, the culprits returned to admire their work. Standing ten yards from the backdoor of my house, the infamous desperado: *Odocoileus hemionus*. The black-tailed deer.

Gardening enemies come in various sizes. And anytime gardening folk get together, the conversation inevitably turns to pesky critters or weather or any number of possible conundrums awaiting anyone devoted to nature and plants. Moles, aphids, dogs and cats, rabbits, squirrels, raccoons, even clumsy neighbor children. But the worst, I decided on that day, are black-tailed deer.

Deer are unabashed. They possess a malevolent quality starkly in contrast with their graceful and mesmerizing presence. I ran out into the backyard to bellow and scream and, hopefully, unnerve them. I tried insults, casting aspersions on their pedigree and their upbringing, and even resorted to the well-worn stab about their mothers and army boots. It was to no avail. They retreated some twenty yards to the edge of a forested area delineated by a wire fence on my neighbor's property. The deer stood utterly still, and we stared at one another in this standoff. I blinked first. And I confess that I was in awe of my new archenemy, lucky to be alive to tell them how beautiful they were, all the while berating them for their impudence, wondering how much they heard and what, if anything, they would remember.

Yesterday there was a family of deer on the road near our driveway. I stopped to watch. Two stayed, motionless, staring back at me. Another bounded in front of the car to woods on the other side. It is disarming, this otherworldly gracefulness, so elegant and engaging, without any apparent effort. For just a moment, it made me want to forgive and forget. To enjoy their company. So intriguing. So enchanting. What is there to hate?

Yet, like thieves in the night they come. Every so often we see them, never alone, always in a group of three to seven, our own neighborhood gang of hooligans, ambling through our backyard at twilight. They have two speeds while in the garden, dally and dawdle, as they stop to enjoy vegetable greens, rose shoots, the leaves and twigs on the young apple trees, or, if all else fails, the tips of carnations.

Even so, their presence is soothing. Soothing because black-tailed deer seem never to be in a hurry. Their meandering, both graceful and gentle, serves as a tranquilizer, which is, I have no doubt, a calculated part of their scheme. And when they stare, heads erect, ears upright as finely tuned antennae, they are statues of polished marble. Under the placid exterior lurks—lest we forget—the nefarious nemesis to roses. My roses. My nemesis. This is, after all, very personal, and when the mix includes deer and roses, there is no room for negotiation or compromise. There is only one option, even for a pacifist: justifiable war.

To battle! I armed myself with every suggestion and wives' tale and country prescription. First it was the commercial spray. "For deer and rabbits," it advertised. Grateful that at last I had found a solution to my dilemma, I raced home to let this elixir do its work, expecting that deer would intuitively panic and raise their tails as flags of surrender.

Technology is not without its concessions. The spray is a white milky substance that leaves its mark, a mark much like spattered paint. So, it was deer or the tie-dyed rosebush look. What a tradeoff. Even so, I was determined, and I faithfully applied this guarantee against varmints, a priest sprinkling some protective holy water on his congregation.

The remedy lasted for about two months. I suspect that the deer were humoring me. For after two months, they began to munch as before. No doubt it tasted to them like some cheap blue-cheese dressing.

There's a man down the road who has surrounded his property with an eight-foot, wire-mesh fence. It does the trick—no deer to be seen—but I've not yet resigned myself to the appearance of a maximum security prison.

"Buy a dog," one local suggested. "That'll take care of your problem."

We had one already. But she was old and not given to exertion, regardless of the cause. So we found a younger brother for her. Conroy was full of boundless energy. I had high hopes.

One morning, the gang strolled through what they presumed to be their turf (something about squatter's rights). As we stood watching from the back patio, I instructed Conroy to "get 'em." He seemed excited, but for reasons that escaped me. He looked at me, looked at the deer, and wondered what all the fuss was about.

"Go," I repeated in my sternest voice. "Do your job. Chase 'em. Scare 'em. Do something. Do anything."

He did. He bounced around, apparently thinking that it was mealtime. I took matters into my own hands.

"Here," I yelled, "watch me."

I grabbed Conroy by the collar and hauled him toward the deer. They stood twenty yards from us, watching this man lug a dog in their direction. I began to chase them, waving my arms.

"Follow me," I shouted back at Conroy. "Do what I do."

He stood in place, staring. The deer retreated into the woods, and one young buck doubled over with laughter.

Next we tried soap. Deer are not especially fond of Irish Spring, we were told.

You've got to wonder whether deer gather somewhere in the woods just to gossip about what the two-legged wonders are trying now:

"It was soap."

"Soap? You're kiddin' me."

"Nope. You should have seen him, traipsing around the garden before the sun was up, hanging bars of soap from tree branches, the whole yard looking like some late-'70s Christmas gala."

"What kind of soap?" one of the younger deer asks.

"They call it Irish Spring," in deer brogue, followed by hysterics all around.

It has been said that gardening is not for the young, because they are not able to handle death. It makes sense.

I confess that I had a different perspective when I lived in Southern California. Because there are no seasons, there is no natural downtime. And, as mentioned earlier, death was dealt with by replacement, treating all plants as annuals, pulled when they showed the slightest decline. When the geraniums got leggy or the salvia wilted or the mums dropped their blooms, it was replacement time. I would remind each plant, as I placed it in the garden, "Do well, or else. There's always more where you came from."

Underneath my manic need, for whatever reason, was a denial of the death that comes with gardening. Like it or not, it just does.

We can, if we wish, chalk it all up to that silly but indefatigable hope that any effort worthwhile will exact little consequence from us. As if we can go about our business unscathed. Perhaps it is time to pay the piper on this one. We need a new federal government warning on any and all herbage: *Gardening is not recommended for the faint at heart, for whatever can happen will. Gardening may be hazardous to your emotional well-being.*

I had hoped, after all, back in my early forays into garden life, only to plant some vegetables. I didn't count on altered emotional states. Like the time I went tiptoeing out in my pajamas with a flashlight, hoping for a surprise attack on the slugs that had been gulping my lettuce, and was struck by the way the dew glistened on the paper-thin leaves. Or lying in bed at two in the morning listening to the fifth straight night of rain on my roof, fearing its adverse effect, when I was calmed by the sound of the leaves of the maple trees accompanying with soft percussion. Or hanging out of the upstairs bathroom window, thinking I could catch the deer in their act but instead noticing the intricate shadows fall and stir on the patio flagstone below, and hearing my voice catch.

It's not just death at stake here. It's the way we've been taught to handle grief. Or loss of any kind, for that matter. I guess you could say that we're not good at loss.

I am a pet lover. As I write this, Graham, one of our beloved cats, is gone. Has been gone now for seven days. "Not long enough to worry yet," concerned friends tell us. Nonetheless, there is a place in my heart that restricts, closes down, not ready to live with another loss.

Gone. A strange euphemism. Meaning dead and gone. Gone, I presume, to heaven. *Gone to* is somehow meant to neutralize *gone from*. But formulas, those born of reason or prayer, never seem to pan out, except in someone else's story. And even then, you wonder.

I miss Graham's swaggered gait. The air of self-confidence, ownership, and immodesty. The sureness in his stare. In this house, he was liege and sovereign.

I miss the playfulness. The unabashed fervor and animation in each pounce and tussle. I miss his stalking Kundera (one of our other cats), stopping, sizing his opponent, two wrestlers vigilant, watching for the first lapse in concentration. Then the slight cock of the head, a half-body twist and lunge. The fight, usually consisting of Kundera graciously consenting to letting Graham work out his aggression, has begun. I miss the tenderness. His touch-activated motor, revved in appreciation, lulling and soothing. A comforting reminder. Graham was my buddy, my pal, my main man.

My difficulty comes from the cultural assumption that even grief must be efficiently and valiantly choreographed. Even in sorrow, we must carry ourselves as a model of decorum (as if made for TV), teardrops and words appropriate, precise. Which leaves the problem that all real feelings pale against such criteria, sounding feeble, inarticulate, imprecise, somehow unauthentic, forced, inadequate. So maybe it is better to keep it inside. Get a new cat and move on, someone told me. I hope not. Not that I know a better way, except that maybe I shouldn't fight so hard to pretend it doesn't hurt. And just let it be.

In our garden shed I keep a coffee can, a depository for plant tags, from plants that didn't make it. They, for one reason or another, passed on to that great garden in the sky. Well, it's not a small can anymore. There is a tag for *Erigeron* 'Moerheim,' an airy flower with daisylike blooms, perfectly spilling out of a rock crevice. And one for *Salvia* 'Indigo Spires,' with its elegant four-foot wands of deep murky purple blooms. The coffee can is my own war memorial, with names like *Diascia cordata, Nepeta tuberosa, Phlox divaricata, Lobelia sessilifolia, Eupatorium chinensis; Alstroemeria psittacina,* with its bizarrely appealing flowers of red-green; *Artemesia* 'Powis Castle,' *Verbena rigida, Jasminum nudiflorum,* and *Ceanothus veitchianus,* names which require no common term translation to get the gist; that, in a small way, it all feels like losing a friend.

It's quite a collection. Some went without much fanfare. Others fought bravely. An unexpected late frost. A nasty windstorm. Or the result of some unnameable infirmity. Some are merely a perpetual reminder of my stubbornness. *Cosmos atrosanguineus,* the

Chocolate Cosmos (it really does smell irresistibly like a Hershey bar), should probably be grown as an annual. I know better. I don't take cuttings or move the plant under a cold frame. I leave it to the elements, and for the past three years, the elements have won. Each spring, another plant tag goes into the coffee can, and I optimistically order another cosmos.

Maybe it puts the whole enterprise into some perspective. For as long as I garden, there will always be that coffee can.

It's not an easy notion to embrace. There is that perpetual and eternal hope (expectation?) for some kind of culmination, the garden intact and complete in its splendor. This insidious demand doesn't allow you to sit on your deck without making mental plans for rearranging or tearing the whole thing out and starting from scratch. Granted, mental monkeying comes with the gardening disease. You fiddle and futz. You guess and gamble. I know now that freedom only comes when we can see that our fiddling is not just a symptom. It is, in fact, the whole idea.

Gardening, after all, is not some place to arrive. It has to do with the direction we are going. Which means that your garden doesn't have to be complete, or without blemish. It doesn't even have to be close. It just has to feel like it's your own, your own little slice of bliss.

In our paranoia over what's missing, or what's not quite right, we forget the solace and medicinal quality of our garden until hours after we've left it. Say, for example, you are numbed, slogging through an airport, bombarded with the panoply of sights and sounds afforded by our modern technology. Neon-lighted sallow faces, departure times squawked over distorted loudspeakers, each announcement knifing through an indomitable din, and the ballyhoo of headlines on newsstand magazines—everything I needed to know about the latest "wait 'till you read this" sex scandal.

So, you sit down. Just for a minute. And then you remember the garden in morning light, around 6:30 that very morning, when, armed with salt, you went to battle slug legions, all this before you were yanked away for God-knows-whatever business.

And you remember the heady fragrance of the rose arbor: 'Seagull,' 'New Dawn,' and 'Trier.' The velvet lilac color of *Penstemon* 'Midnight,' rising out of a clump of bellflowers, backed by the nodding white blooms of the damask rose 'Madame Hardy.' All of this tempered by mourning the loss of a trio of Madonna lilies, slug-slaughtered, their buds all but gone. Tempered, yes, but not erased. For while you are muttering and shaking your head, you notice the dewdrops on the evergreen huckleberry and a robin playing tug-of-war with a morning worm. They go together, these extremes. They are inexorably and wonderfully intertwined.

Gardening is an exasperating way of life, but only if we expected some intended result, needing our garden or landscape to conform to some predetermined goal. And it's not just the garden we're talking about. Any issue relating to the good life, personal growth, and the soul is suffocated by demanding some pre-arranged goal.

I confess that I don't remember much from graduate school, save one quote from my theology professor, Ray Anderson. "Spirituality," he would tell us, "is the ability to live with ambiguity." That was news to me—to that young man doing his best to play the right notes.

I know now that Dr. Anderson was reminding us that spirituality means learning a willingness to embrace life—*this* life—in all of its imperfections. Spirituality is, in fact, not some predetermined destination, but the direction we are going.

Like it or not, loss and any consequent change is essential to a garden. An ingredient we do our best to chase from the garden. As if there's some arrival point when we can finally say, "We've done it."

It's a notion to evict from our cranial basket of worries—the sooner, the better. Or it may infect all the other areas of our life, with the crazy hope of some arrival. And then we live like four-year-old children, five minutes out of the driveway on any family trip. "Are we there yet?"

"Are we there yet?" in translation can mean "the garden is almost where I want it to be." Meaning that I hope it will stay put for the photo opportunity. Of course, this year my hosta and carex bed is a mass of bleeding hearts and *Linaria purpurea*. And my peony bed has been taken over by an overly aggressive salal shrub. Oh, it is all lovely in its own way, but certainly not the way I had it planned.

Calvin, of "Calvin and Hobbes" fame, is always bemoaning the fact that character building invariably attaches itself to unpleasant experiences. I'm with Calvin on this one. When unpleasantness— loss, calamity, tragedy—strikes, there's a knee-jerk need to make sense of it. Contain it, analyze it, and come up with a pithy moral to the story. Apparently it gives some aura of solace, knowing that our discomfort was not for naught. Who knows, we may even be able to market our newfound insights and garner the acclaim needed to offset any inconvenience.

I'm not so sure about such mental gymnastics, as if we are incapable of suffering loss without a lesson learned. It reminds me of an old episode of *Barney Miller*. Wojo, one of the police officers in Barney Miller's precinct, had shot and killed a man in the line of duty. He was disconsolate. Other members of the force tried in a variety of ways to help Wojo get over his depression. Some passed it off with attempts at humor in an effort to cheer him up. Others philosophized about it. Some, in a more hard-nosed fashion, just urged him to get on with life. No one was able to help.

Barney was leaving the office at the end of the day. Wojo was still sitting at his desk. As Barney was about to leave, he turned to Wojo and said, "Did you know that the largest mammal in the world is the sperm whale?"

"No," said Wojo, looking puzzled.

"So, you know how large its throat is?"

"No."

Lifting his arm and holding his thumb and index finger about two inches apart, he said, "About this big."

"Oh."

"And do you know why that is?"

"No."

"Because that's the way it is, and there's nothing you can do about it."

So, I retire to my back deck on a May evening when the sun is still high in the southwestern sky, and admire my new unplanned bevy of bleeding hearts. There's a pair of black-headed Grosbeaks at the feeder, the male with its rusty orange collar and the female with its black and white face paint, munching on black, oiled sunflower seeds. I am comforted by their company, and they seem content to munch without my need to dazzle them with insight.

I called a name listed on the Seattle Rose Society's register of rose experts. From his voice, I judged him to be in the neighborhood of seventy, his voice grandfatherly in its unhurried tone, not at all put on, with no hint of impatience that there were more or better things to do than talk to this newly arrived city boy, hoping to make good in the country.

I told him about my problem with the deer. And then recounted my litany of attempted recipes, telling him that my backyard still smells of Irish Spring.

"Oh, I've tried all that, too," he chuckled. And then added, "They say that lion dung works, but I've never run across any to try it."

"Got any other ideas?" I asked.

There was a pause. "What you need, you have in unlimited supply," he told me as if winking.

I bit. "What's that?"

"Urine," he told me.

"Excuse me?" I tried to sound polite.

And he laughed again. A knowing laugh. "Deer don't come near human urine."

Since my first encounters with deer, I have moved twice, beginning new garden adventures. Now that we live high on a knoll, the deer seem to leave us alone. Even so, over the years I've developed a habit that's been hard to break. To this day, I pee around my rose bushes. I suppose there's got to be a lesson in here somewhere. I realize that this option is not possible on Third and Main with your neighbors watching. Unless you can convince them that it's an ancient religious ceremony. But you might try telling them you're a gardener. That seems to explain everything.

# SOUL GARDENING EXERCISES

## *Magnificent Heartbreaks*

If you have a garden—flower or vegetable—find a coffee can you can use for plant tags. Save every tag from those plants that have died or succumbed to the elements.

What is there about our culture that steers clear of death and grief—untidiness? What is there about us that requires neat and uncluttered conclusions? What is the reason that so many of us seek an immediate replacement—a substitute—for whatever we have lost?

"Nothing can make up for the absence of someone whom we loved, and it would be wrong to try to find a substitute; we must simply hold out and see it through. That sounds very hard at first, but at the same time it is a great consolation, for the gap, as long as it remains unfilled, preserves the bonds between us. It is nonsense to say that God fills the gap; he does not fill it, but on the contrary, he keeps it empty and so helps us to keep alive our former communion with each other, even at the cost of pain" (Dietrich Bonhoeffer, *Letters and Papers from Prison*). Why are we so eager to have these gaps filled? What are the benefits to keeping them empty?

*Quote for the day: "You need chaos in your soul to give birth to a dancing star" (Friedrich Nietzsche).*

# WINTER

---

*To sit still, and listen . . .*
*To gasp and feel lucky to be alive*

# SEVEN

## A QUIET MIND—WINTER'S RELEASE

*[Green thoughts] emerge from some deep source of stillness*
*which the very fact of winter has released.*
—Mirabel Osler

*Turn down the noise. Reduce the speed. Be like the somnolent bears,*
*or those other animals that slow down and almost die in the cold season.*
*Let it be the way it is. The magic is there in its power.*
—Henry Mitchell

I am headed off island on a winter morning during the week before Christmas day. It is winter solstice. The nighttime temperatures are close enough to the magical freezing point to leave the landscape as a glazed pen-and-ink drawing, shadowed with white pencil. To the east, a gold band of sunlight is trapped beneath a bulky cloud layer, just above an ink-black horizon. Off the starboard of our ferry, four sea lions loll and romp, spooling through the water. Their bark, like a stone tossed across the swells, skips through the morning stillness.

To the west, the Olympic Mountain snowcapped peaks float as apparitions in the dusk shadows. It is a dream landscape, one of dreams lost and buried. I stand on deck at the railing, hypnotized by the mountains and the sheer arresting scale of this panorama.

Outside of an occasional barking sea lion, or the clank of the ferry ramp as a late car boards, the air is still. Very still. Whatever need I had to rush loses its momentum. I let miscellaneous thoughts settle.

I feel weighted, anchored to the railing. Perhaps this is the right for-mula for dreams that have been lost to slowly, slowly emerge.

To be sure, winter does not easily evoke emerging dreams. Or quiet respites gazing at sunrises. Here in the Northwest, winter means high waders or duck boots, slogging over (and through) saturated soil. It means rain-streaked horizons, leaky roofs, and muddy cars. It means short days and blue moods vented with a periodic and requisite nervous breakdown.

My own winter garden is sodden and tired and weary. Artemesias lay clumped as a pile of wadded laundry. Spent and decomposing aster stalks sprawl like an abandoned game of pick-up sticks. And the aftermath of the hardy geraniums passes for a pile of shredded wet paper towels. For those enamored by prim and tidy and glossy, such a scene is sure to disappoint. Especially this year. After a record rainfall in November and December and January and February, we are now, officially, a wetland that stretches from Oregon to the Canadian border. Tourists are encouraged to bring canoes.

Some people who do visit me during the winter expect some-thing different. And they want, of course, to see the garden.

"Why don't you landscape this area?" One visitor asked, pre-suming to be helpful.

This is probably not the time to tell him how many months it took to get this area to look like this, at least not without bran-dishing a garden rake for emphasis.

"What is it you see in this kind of garden anyway?" the espe-cially bold will interrogate. As if I am either terribly eccentric, or one slice short of a loaf.

Walking people through your winter garden is not unlike introducing yourself at an important event when you have the flu.

One can hardly expect anything but knowing smiles, oozing pity, and well-wishes.

"Not much to see here, is there?" One visitor asked casually.

I swallowed hard. "True," I wanted to say, "but I guess that all depends on what you are looking for. . . ."

For if you look up, you will see the filigreed canopy created by our 150-foot cedar tree. Or off to the side, notice the mottled rust bark of our native madrone tree, revealing, like a shedding skin, a trunk with the polished gleam of a cinnamon swizzle stick. Or admire the dark, rich green of our native yew, covered with red-hot tinged berries resembling miniature pitted olives. Or be amazed by the fronds of licorice fern, a pendant from the trunks of big-leaf maple trees and woodland rock. Behind our studio is an old concrete cistern. Still in use, licorice fern rings its rim like a Roman wreath. Even so, we're all inculcated, sensing the question still hanging in the air, as a lingering indictment: "So, there's not much to see, is there?"

The disappointment, of course, is real, and you find yourself wishing you could make it up to them. Because it's difficult to explain that real gardens don't work that way. That herbaceous really does imply that all foliage vanishes over the winter—no doubt vacationing somewhere south of here—leaving large vacant patches. We so want the garden to indulge and thrill us nonstop, we miss the obvious fact that gardens need winter just to catch their breath.

We're no different about ourselves, of course, as much as we'd like to think otherwise. Perhaps we are afraid of what stopping—going dormant—implies. Glaring empty space. Implications of nonproductivity and weakness. All leading us down that inevitable spiral toward old age and death—or worse, a cozy room at the "We'll Visit Every Other Sunday Manor House for the Feeble and Nonimportant."

Let's face it. We all have some compulsion to fill our time.

I have participated in several retreat weekends at a Benedictine monastery. It involved clergy and other "important" busy people. During coffee breaks, there was always a long line of attendees jockeying for the one and only pay phone (this being prior to cellular), as if it assured some connection with real life, namely, what we do. Now we walk around with phones as if they were permanently attached to our ears. We fill our Day-Timers as if there was some inescapable race toward something else (or, in the words of Tennessee Williams, we "attempt to find in motion what was lost in space"). Perhaps Alfred E. Neuman was right all these years: "Most of us don't know what we want in life, but we're sure we haven't got it."

*Newsweek* blares its 1995 headline: "Exhausted." I see the trend toward downsizing—cutting back in work, money expectations, and lifestyle. Living simply—I'm in favor. But it takes a conscious effort, apparently acknowledging that the fast lane has no exit ramp.

I saw a big hotel chain advertisement about their "bounceback weekend." A weekend to catch up, slow down, and relax, the ad promised. It makes you wonder what has gone on the other fifty-one weekends that makes this weekend so critical. We easily say we wish for an extra day in our week, not really knowing what to do with the extra hour we have while waiting at the doctor's office.

This pace defines my value as a consumer and a producer, as if everything in life is a test to pass or a contest to win. All the while I am waiting for the right answer or correct advice to bring an end to any downtime so that my normal life can be resumed.

In an interview about a recent album, Donna Summer talked about her long layoff from singing:

It's hard to explain to anybody that's searching for this kind of fame, but it's a lot of work. You do it, but you don't really enjoy it. I use this analogy: When you plant a garden, every certain number of years you have to let it alone to let the soil replenish itself. We all need some downtime. Unfortunately, the music industry isn't geared to health; it's geared to tonnage.

I understand the pressure. After ten years in a job that required travel forty weekends out of each year, I stopped. There was only one problem. I had no idea what to do with my time.

Winter does us a favor. Here in the Northwest we don't often get severe winter weather. So when we do—temperature in the teens, roads iced and insurmountable —things pretty much come to a halt. Our canyon driveway makes it impossible to drive, which means you hunker down on the couch, blanket on your lap and cup of tea in hand, and let the silence descend while you survey the whitecaps out on Puget Sound.

It has been said that when the supports are gone, we can find where our real worth lies. Not exactly what we may have had in mind, but so it is. In his book entitled *Transitions,* William Bridges calls this time the neutral zone. It is an essential stage on our journey, but easily misunderstood. The neutral zone is the invitation to stop, to listen, to take a deep breath, and to take inventory, and by so doing, nurture the soul. That is another way of saying it is an invitation to hunker down and chew the cud, to ruminate, with no need to come up with any answers because none are required.

It is an invitation seldom taken, because to stop may mean facing some discomfort. Like remembering decisions we wish the hell we hadn't made. Or facing the reality that our position in the race of life is farther back than we had hoped. But the truth is that after all our moaning and moping, we come one day to enjoy our own company, and start to look forward to those slivers of winter, embracing the reality that we are, after all, human. And that is not such a bad place to be.

Temptations to do without any neutral zone are as persistent as our June mosquitoes. One temptation insinuates that any such downtime is sure to be morose. Not to mention boring. We conjure up images of an emergency ward for emotional invalids. It is always accompanied by an incessant taped voice, nasal and edged with an imputed third degree, pressing, "Are you going to just sit there, and do . . . nothing!?"

It's so easy to feel the barb of guilt from that tape and buy into the temptation that downtime can surely wait until we have the time to really appreciate it. Say, maybe next month. Or certainly the month after. Or there's the temptation to see all of this as optional behavior, apparently suited to those with an appropriate temperament. After all, some of us are not downtime people. So, it must be genetic.

Lucy and Peppermint Patty were lying lazily beside a tree, carrying on a conversation. "Do they have prayer in your school?" Peppermint Patty asked.

"No," Lucy answered. "But last year they had us observe a 'moment of silence.'"

"How did that work?" Peppermint Patty asked.

Lucy replied, "It almost killed me!"

When I tell people that I live on a very secluded knoll, they immediately wonder, "What do you do?" conjuring images of either some ancient hermitage or a wacky cult, as if life apart from the adjacent comfort of neon lights is unthinkable.

Whenever I do bring up this subject, it is nigh impossible to get around the inevitable, "Well, what do you *do* during this downtime?"

It is as if this downtime is timed, and an accounting is required by the headmaster, complete with written accomplishments and goals. It may be hard to swallow, but the truth is, what you *do* is irrelevant.

The Jewish tradition calls downtime Sabbath. It is a day (or season) for the herbaceous distractions, "to do" lists, and obligations to die back. A day of rest. Actually, the literal translation would be more like, "the day to do nothing." So, I guess it's not what you do but what you *don't do* that really matters here. Which means that it is a time without need for justification. Plain and simple: just go into the innermost chamber of your soul and shut the door. A healthy garden has a Sabbath. A healthy soul is no different.

In his poem "The Spiritual Canticle," St. John of the Cross describes God as "music without a sound, sonorous solitude." Charles Cummings talks about John's commentary in his book *The Mystery of the Ordinary:*

> (John points) out that the divine music can best be heard in solitude and silence. The sonorous music is not a physical sound that vibrates the eardrum but something transcending the senses. Physical solitude and silence remove the distracting noises that prevent us from hearing on deeper levels. John of the Cross was a strong advocate of disciplining or "emptying" the external senses as well as the memory, intellect, and will, so as to open other levels of sensitivity within the self. "Openness to the divine music that is heard without a sound" provides an elaborate description of the experience of praying. In simpler terms, prayer is listening.

This makes good sense to me. Prayer and solitude are good partners in the garden. And, I may hear nothing, or I may hear God's voice on a gentle breeze.

Winter gives us another gift, because it allows us to see the bones of the garden, those plants or rocks or structures that give the garden space its essential shape and character. Such elements provide a border, or a boundary. They are the ingredients for a design, or the weaving of a story. More often than not, color and flowers can get in the way. During winter, there is no tangle or profusion of summer blooms to cover the bare and telling spots. Lines and border contours that gladly played a supporting role, receding into the landscape when spring and summer begin their pageant, enjoy their moment in the foreground, now well defined and prominent.

Perhaps winter conflicts with our cultural bias, namely, that production equals value—dictating that even downtime must have some benefit. Otherwise, what's its purpose? So if we're going to stop, we want to do it correctly. As if there is a manual to follow. Either that, or stopping conjures images of emptying—unloading—our mind, creating a large airy room that proves we've attained a higher spiritual plane, allowing us to look down at busy hurried people with pinched and knowing smiles. But downtime isn't about emptying so much as it is about getting reacquainted.

I remember the one and only time my dad took me deer hunting. My father loved deer hunting, meaning he loved his annual pilgrimage to Michigan's Upper Peninsula, where my grandfather used to go and my great-grandfather before him. It was the same place every year, the forest a thicket, a wild and luxuriant fur covering the back of this continent.

There were five and us, and we would hunt from mid-morning until dusk. *Hunt,* in my case, meant parking my butt near a tree where I was deposited by my father, maybe six hundred yards from camp, 30-30 lever action on my lap, waiting, I suppose, for some deer to blunder my way.

On the second day, I fired a shot into a large maple just so the others wouldn't think what was true—that I did sit by a tree all day. Or maybe I did it to feel the kick of the rifle butt on my shoulder, as some initiation to manhood that throbbed the remainder of the day. After the report, the silence rendered everything in slow motion, and I saw a frightened doe glide among the weighed boughs of young spruce coated with snow. She stopped to stare, somehow intuiting that I would not fire again. I could smell the powder from the gun, and the deer looked at me with liquid brown eyes that sensed something I was afraid to know.

A pressure valve had been released, and all striving ceased. The remainder of the day passed slowly. It was as if my small area of woods had been sealed off from the rest of the world, now a world all mine. I became keenly aware of the silence and my isolation. I listened to my breath and felt my heartbeat. Time slowed, and dreams shook off their hibernation and floated to the surface. I spun stories in my mind, and traveled to other lands. And I passed some time during that afternoon entertaining the wildlife, practicing for an upcoming piano recital, using the barrel of my gun laid across my lap as an imaginary keyboard. When I walked back to camp, the snow crunched under my boots, and the thick stillness of the forest felt palpable.

I took some time during our last winter storm to read *Moments in Eden,* by Richard Brown, and *Visions in Paradise,* by Marina Schinz, both tantalizing volumes of photographs, of gardens and vistas that mesmerize, evoke, and send the mind off on some waking dream. I particularly enjoyed those segments about the garden in winter. Letting the garden be without any attempt to give it zest or a facelift.

All of these reminders reinforce the disquieting disclaimer that

This is, to be sure, difficult to do without some ulterior motive, still seeing the whole bit as a self-help project with recognizable steps and a guaranteed return on investment. We still want to make downtime work. As in accomplish something. It can't help but cry out for a pithy motto, such as Solitude for Sanity or Interlude for Inner Peace.

There's the catch. We demand a payoff in all of this. There must be something in this for me, or why mess with it? It's just that the payoff may not be as we expected or hoped, or in evidence as advertised.

I have a friend whose father used to respond to the question, "What are you doing?" with a pause, a puff on his pipe, and the drawn-out reply, "How soon do you need to know?"

When I lived in Southern California, I spent time every six weeks at the Benedictine monastery. The monastery is two hours out of Los Angeles in the high desert. My first times at the monastery were sprinkled liberally with second thoughts and disappointment. What I had hoped for was a quiet weekend, no obligations, no pressure, just two days to kick back, read a book, sleep in, take a nap, take a walk, enjoy the sunset. I remember sitting on the patio outside my room, smoking my pipe (a requisite adornment for every graduate student). The sun had passed behind the mountains, now a bruised purple. I looked at my watch. There was another three hours to kill before bedtime. What to do. My normal distractions were not available to me here. There was no television, movie theater, or telephone.

But what had I expected? That I could come face-to-face with me without having to face the lifestyle which put me in a pickle in the first place? (I am reminded of the movie Round Midnight, a piece based on the life of a jazz saxophonist tormented by a lifestyle of self-destruction. In the film, it is the saxophonist's hope—conscious or not—to find some place where he could outrun the torment. "I'm going to Paris," he tells a friend, "to play the clubs there for awhile." "You can go to Paris," his friend replies. "But do you know who you'll meet when you get off the plane in Paris? You.") For all my posturing, it evidently was not enough just to sit, smoke my pipe, and ponder the moon.

Fifty yards or so from the guest house, one of the older monks had created a garden space, using eucalyptus trees as a buffer against sun and wind. The effect was a cool—even on the hottest of summer days—secluded place, with a bench and a grassy patch ideal for napping. You entered the space through a pergola cloaked by hardy shrub roses. The temperature dropped perceptibly, as if the parched air had been siphoned off, and you soon found yourself flopped on the ground, drifting off while looking up through the eucalyptus branches. Slowly but surely, the dust of shame could be shaken off, and you came to relish your downtime. As one visitor to the garden reported, "It feels like my life has been saved, and I wasn't even aware of any danger. Solitude as necessity, demandable, honorable. Not sinful, indulgent, wasteful, undeserved."

The etymology of *garden* suggests an enclosure, although its boundaries may be more psychological than physical. It means that the garden is not merely a place of plants, but a protected place. Looking back, only now do I see my small corner of a northern Michigan woodland as a special garden.

It goes back to seeing the garden as something less tangible than flowering cosmos, or lanky pole beans. I read a story in *US News and World Report* of the San Francisco Garden Project. Cathy Sneed, the project's founder, helps turn neglected areas into garden spaces, using labor from San Francisco prisons:

Most of Sneed's pupils have never held a job. If they ever planted a tomato or turned a shovelful of earth, it was long ago, a dim memory of childhood. And in the garden, [the protected place], they begin to rediscover themselves. Next to a bed of lettuce, a woman in a blue kerchief kneels, her face flushed from weeding. A few months ago, she was serving time for possessing heroin. Now she has discovered lilacs and spinach, Calendula and Algerminium. She may not be one of those who make it, returning, instead, to a world of seamy hotel rooms. But for once, she voices a cautious optimism: "Seeing garbage turn into something pretty gives me something. Maybe by the grace of God, I'll blossom someday."

The winter garden helps by inviting us to do the inner work. Walking, feeding birds, watching the snow or rain, sitting by the fire, petting our cat, building sandcastles in our dreams, counting stars, sipping coffee, taking a long bath, perusing seed catalogs, daydreaming, waiting for God-knows-what to happen, living with two essential ingredients while sitting still, namely, attentive inactivity and ritualized routine—all the while, vaguely aware of the frenzied gardener lurking in the recesses of our minds. "There's not much to see here, is there?"

For me, it is early morning. I have finished walking our two dogs. Snow and ice still cling to the grass pathway. The air smells crisp and clean. I meander around, a morning roll call. I see the resolute blades of our bearded iris—in summer, with falls of violet, one we call 'Grandma's Mystery'—remembering its refreshing fragrance of French-milled soap. I see the swollen stems of *Iris reticulata,* and the raisin-sized hips suspended from the canes of *Rosa gymnocarpa.* I decide to sit for a minute on the wooden bench perched on our back deck. Every once in a while, the air is pierced by the cackle of a pileated woodpecker or the bark of a neighborhood dog.

I have a friend who works part-time. By choice. She likes her job, and it affords her alone time. Even so, people persist in asking, "Can't you find a real job?" Oddly enough, we seem threatened by anyone who dares to take downtime.

There's a story about a woman who was going through some life transition and loss. She decided to spend four days, in the spirit of the Australian aborigine "walkabouts," backpacking alone in the mountains. "Where can we reach you?" her husband asked with concern. The woman, who had never gone anywhere by herself, replied simply, "You can't. But I'll be back."

By the time our ferry reaches the West Seattle dock, the sun has seeped through, giving the snow-capped Olympics a burnished sheen. The dock sounds blend and fill the air: seagulls calling, the slap of water against the boat, voices carrying across the ferry deck. My mind is brought back to the day at hand and the relentless list of items needing my attention. I take a deep breath and one long last look back across the sound toward Blake Island and the illumined western horizon.

# SOUL GARDENING EXERCISES

## A Quiet Mind—Winter's Release

Take a mini Sabbath. Say, one hour or half a day. Plan blessed nothing. Leave your phone and pager locked in a drawer, and throw away the key. This is a time on your calendar to sit still. A "Sabbath" date," "Red-X Time" again. Take out your calendar and intentionally mark off time with a red X. There's no need to be terribly compulsive about it. Begin with fifteen minutes. The options are limitless: Ensconced in an Adirondack chair listening to Vivaldi's "Four Seasons," walking the beach, hiking the mountains, praying the psalms, enjoying a picnic at the local park, taking a drive through the countryside, strolling through a farmer's market.

Pay attention to sounds. Notice what we are tuned to hear. And notice what sounds we have learned to tune out. Notice the background noises we learn to tolerate. Think about the role these noises play—bombarding and barraging and cascading, and shutting out silence.

Find a place where you can listen to silence. Literally. What's it like? Why does silence threaten us so? What are the messages we receive from our culture about silence?

Try to go through a day without your Day-Timer or beeper or cell phone or computer, or watch. Notice how much lighter you already feel.

*Quote for the day: "God is not attained by a process of addition to anything in the soul, but by a process of subtraction" (Meister Eckhart).*

# EIGHT

## ENCHANTMENT AND GOOSEFLESH

*Where, alas, is seduction and gooseflesh on the arms?*
—Mirabel Osler

*Almost the whole world is asleep. Only a few people are awake, and they live in a state of constant total amazement.*
—Joe versus the Volcano

"When I first came here," she tells me, "I was enchanted." We are sitting on our deck, looking down through the evergreen swale of Cedarhurst Canyon. Our line of sight takes us out over Fern Cove, the mouth of Shinglemill Creek, straight for Blake Island, with the Kitsap Peninsula painted over its western shoulder. It is spring. From this angle, the canyon is a Russell Chatham oil on expanded canvas: scattered big-leaf maples, like smears of honey mustard, on this palate punctured with the deep green steeples of Douglas fir, western hemlock (with their telltale nodding tips), and the sea-green lacework crowns of western red cedar.

"Before I lived here, I used to come up and sit on the deck," my wife tells me. "It has always been medicine to my blue moods."

I believe her.

This medicine is generously meted out in the flight of a red-tailed hawk, the burnished skin and grain of a fallen madrone limb, the visitation of a benign and amiable black bear, the rekindled coral-flame blooms of red currant, and the reoccurring springtime carpet of bunchberry, its blooms a white vigil-light countenance.

Medicine for our blue moods strikes a chord. For this medicine is all about times and places where we can be enchanted. Places to gasp and feel lucky. Times and places to feel gooseflesh on our arms.

I am remembering the time my wife and I traveled to Las Vegas for a business trip. It's easy to demonize the glitz and kitsch. But then, it's not just anywhere that you can be married by Elvis.

I will say this: I was never once alone there. Literally. I mean, I was never once in a place where I could catch my breath, as it were, or my thoughts. There was no place where I wasn't bombarded by din, lights, and ballyhoo. But that's the point. After all, what kind of fun is it without din, lights, and clamor, the sure-fire, three-part recipe for excitement and revelry.

They have their place, say, once a year at the Fat Tuesday parade, when you throw all caution to the wind, say the hell with it, and party without premeditation. Whatever cleanup needs to be done can wait until tomorrow. But this wasn't Fat Tuesday. I was woeful at blackjack, and I had a headache.

On our last day, we drove west on state road 159 toward Red Rock Canyon Recreation Area. In Las Vegas proper, surrounded by inexhaustible glass, relentless fountains, and gemstone green fairways, you can forget, for a moment, that you are, in fact, smack-dab in the middle of a vast desert. One that stretches for miles and miles and miles. What a spectacular wasteland.

You see Red Rock Canyon long before you arrive. You can't help but see it. It rises abruptly above the desert floor, a formation of odd and unquestionable beauty. Somewhere in the neighborhood of 65 million years ago, two plates in earth's crust collided, and a mass of red sandstone ended up sandwiched in between two equally sized masses of suntanned rock. Such a marvel is caused when a fracture in the earth's crust drives one plate over the top of another. As a result, the stone above is older than the stone below.

As you begin to drive what is called the scenic loop, before you find a place to park and explore, you notice that your car has dramatically slowed, as if of its own volition, and you wonder if the air is drugged, for you feel the need to stall, to say nothing, to simply stare in awe. There is the illusion that time has slowed here, receded even, as if history's carousel had been ratcheted back a couple of notches, and when you step out of your car, you momentarily forget where you are. It is the scale of the place, not merely its size, but its elegant grandeur that strikes you. And whatever distractions you brought with you begin to fall away as all of your energy is marshaled into absorbing whatever is around you.

We walked and sat and looked and pointed. We watched families clamber around the sandstone formations—rounded, weathered smooth—the children waving and laughing to their parents below. Some people were sitting alone. Some were painting and sketching. Some were snoozing on blankets perched on the rocks.

You don't spend your hours pulling on slot arms here. On the strip, I watched families stopping to pose for pictures in front of casinos, limousines, and fountains that spouted water higher than building tops. Twenty miles away, here in Red Rock Canyon, there is silence, save for the occasional ricocheting laughter of children mingling with the stream that runs down through the cathedral of primeval stone.

And there is gooseflesh on our arms.

Most such places or moments are notable if only for their ordinariness. Watching as the steam vapor rises from the mid-morning vegetable garden soil, young tomato stalks appear as apparitions in the late spring sunlight. Or standing at the base of the two-hundred-year-old Douglas fir tree only a stone's throw from our deck, its bark deeply furrowed, two friends and I, hands joined, are unable to form a ring around its trunk. Or doing a double take, noticing the bloom on an *Iris chrysographes* for the first time, a diminutive plant with raven black blooms that are arresting and exquisite. Or looking out the bedroom window on a chilly November night, noticing how the moon has coated the upper garden bench in a mercury phosphorescence; this is the light of clandestine lovers, an image done in charcoal and chalk, of nights past when your heart raced with both terror and euphoria, the light lending credibility to your sense that everything on this one night is in focus, clearer and more substantial. Or the time driving home from the golf course a little after five, rounding a corner to behold an enormous saffron globe suspended just above the horizon. It takes you aback as it is so incongruous, this moon looking as close as the nearest mountain range. And you know, right then and there, you are lucky and blessed.

We would do well to learn from the Navajo concept of being blessed—a variation on the concept of the Sacrament of the Present Moment—captured here in a book of poetry by Murray Bodo titled *Walk in Beauty:*

At dawn I walk.
Behind me it is blessed where I walk,
Before me it is blessed where I walk,
I walk, I walk,
At dawn I walk.

In his book *The Mystery of the Ordinary,* Charles Cummings observes that "the Navajo walker is enveloped in blessing. As he explored the beginning of a new day, he felt completely in harmony with the land where he walked and with the mystery that revealed something of itself in the dawn light." Wonder and enchantment were not strangers to the Navajo walker, even to his ordinary days.

Any way you slice it, these places and these moments, they are sacred. Of course, such places I have visited only in my dreams. They are lands where time ceases to exist. There are images— images charged with scents and colors, with shapes and textures. I have such a dream place. And I visit often.

Off the back terrace, there is a rolling terrain. Worn granite steps lead down to a grass path, which creates a visual straight line (some sixty yards) to a rectangular reflecting pool. On either side of the pathway, twelve-foot-wide perennial borders frame the full length of the walkway, plants cascading and spilling over.

It is mid-June in my dream, and the borders are enlarged. The wash of color forms a Monet palate, lavender domes of *Geranium* 'Kashmir Purple' melded with silver lace mounds of *Artemesia* 'Powis Castle,' the floppy habit of *Penstemon glaber,* and the resolute emerald blades of an aster whose time is yet to come. This cluster is flanked by the weighed boughs of 'Comte de Chambord,' its blossoms a silken pink, and its canes mingled with regal delphinium spires and the filigree of bronze fennel.

The air on this late afternoon is filled with the intoxicating confectionery of wallflowers, sensuous as Mediterranean oil. Bees continue to shuttle and scurry. Butterflies float and drift. I pinch a tip of lavender, roll it through my fingers, and hold it to my nose, releasing a smelling salt as essential as vitamin C.

At the back of the eastern border stands a yew hedge with shrubs august and elegant, having been given their head for eighty years. And the western border is backed by a century-old wall of Cotswold stone with unpretentious and graceful lines.

Around the reflector pool are pavers of granite, and a teakwood bench on the far perimeter allows us to look back over the pool through the serene border and on toward the house. Ivy scrambles and shrouds the chimney on the south face of the main house, which carries a medieval and dignified presence, made of ballast stones from old ships. The plum tree has exploded into bloom, its limbs heavy with rain and bowed as if obeisant or weary. The house's south wall is gilded with the climbing roses 'Rambling Rector' and 'Trier.' Near the bench where we sit, I sink my nose into the blooms of the mock orange *Philadelphus* 'Belle Étoile' with its misting perfume erotic and addictive.

Tea and biscuits are served on the reflector pool veranda. Wooly thyme and the lavender bells of campanula spill out from between the crevices and crannies.

Medicine for my blue moods indeed.

I wake from my daydream to the worries of the day, and the relentless hammering of Seattle rain on our metal roof.

So, I'm a dreamer. That my dream garden doesn't actually exist is a bit nitpicky—and, frankly, quite beside the point. For whether it exists or not, there can be no denying the fact that it is real. It is a place where I wander and sit, where I ponder and peruse. A place where I nap and relish, where I gush and effuse. And apparently the place where the fledgling poet in me comes to life.

It brings to mind a recent conversation with a friend—two guys in their early forties doing what guys in their early forties do best: bemoan the loss of hair, virility, and years, and speculate about when life begins. We moved from waxing philosophical about life in general to the more precise theme of what it means to feel alive.

"Is there anything," my friend wondered, "that you feel passionate about?" Such a question is never free from conflicted emotion. After all, does he know something I don't? Is it not okay to show pride in one's passion? Will my gushing smack of boastfulness?

In times like these, the compliant peacekeeper in me shows its mettle. Will others see your passion as misguided? it asks. Followed by seeds of doubt. Is there really a fire burning? And if so, does the object of my passion have value? Oh woe, and more woe!

Even so, internal consternation and all, my answer came surprisingly straightforward, "Gardening. And writing. Hands down."

"Gardening?" he sounded incredulous.

I nodded.

"Gardening," he repeated. "That's your passion? Gardening? Isn't that just a tad self-centered? Shouldn't your passions be others-related?"

Well. I guess I had never thought about it that way. It is true however. Passion itself gives an appearance of self-centeredness. An emotional state of mind best eschewed in favor of accommodation and harmony. For I was raised in a world where one did one's best not to stick out, not to call attention. Passion, like pride, was to be muted. Downplayed. If we had any passions at all, we either allowed others to talk us out of them or kept our mouths shut. It is, no doubt, some quirk of early adolescence that persists, leaving me to easily obsess, preoccupied about what anyone around me thinks about me. Any hobbies or passions or fantasies or curious yearnings can be suppressed in favor of dreaded public opinion.

Gardening is not a luxury or hobby that is added to the list of other projects in our lives. Some résumé item. To be a gardener is not just something you pick up to fill weekends. It is not even something you do, but something done unto you.

Ironically, it was when I came to the realization that I had indeed—no turning back—become a gardener, that I felt fully out of my "self." As in "non-self-centered." As in "non-self-conscious." For at stake was a connectedness to something much larger than my own petty issues. Even in the planting of a row of nasturtiums alongside my first adult attempt at a vegetable garden, with carrots, lettuce, and cucumber, came an involvement in a world much bigger than the peculiar little affairs of my life. My garden placed me squarely in a world of sun and moon, wind and rain, soil and water, insects and animals, summer and winter, germination and death, personal responsibility and Sabbath.

Gardening is a passion that made me want to care, to really give a damn about this slice of the planet entrusted to me. Caring about things that had never occurred to me before——water tables and pesticides and safe food; clear-cutting and erosion; trees, forests, and open spaces; places preserved for public sanctuary and future generations. For once, all of it mattered. It really mattered.

In the end, I wanted to walk my friend through the garden of my dreams. I wanted to tell him about my own journey and that point of conversion that led me to a new world where light and shade dance and cavort, and time itself expands to make space for glory on earth.

That is, a part of me did.

And a part of me decided to let it go.

There's something in the telling that dilutes. There is too much pretense to overcome, knowing that such stories are often related for favor and gain, as just another means to score some points and make an impression. Even so, it still all boils down to what we want to be when we grow up——and if we can be comfortable being a real and living person with passion, oblivious to the need for others to validate our existence.

There is another corollary, and that has to do with the way we see God's connection to this journey. I have never been big on arguing for God's existence or getting in much of a tizzy with those who felt determined to convince me God never existed in the first place. I'll leave that argument for those who apparently have a good deal of time on their hands.

My concern had to do with how God fit into the scheme. You see, I was raised in a church world that preached sermons about a transcendent deity—a God all-powerful and all-knowing and all-seeing. A deity, as far as I could tell, who had nothing whatsoever to do with my world. Because I never once heard a sermon about what is at the core of the Christian faith—and that is an immanent deity, a God who has immersed himself into our world, a God who is *with us*. It is the God Paul Tillich calls "the Ground of All Being." With this God, the consequence is clear: Behind me it is blessed where I walk, and before me it is blessed where I walk. The result is eloquently worded in Joshua Abraham Heschel's prayer:

> Dear Lord, grant me the grace of wonder. Surprise me, amaze me, awe me in every crevice of your universe. Delight me to see how your Christ plays in ten thousand places, lovely in limbs, and lovely in eyes not his, to the Father through the features of men's faces. Each day enrapture me with your marvelous things without number. I do not ask to see the reason for it all; I ask only to share the wonder of it all.

There are ways that this culture can lull you to sleep if you aren't careful and don't occasionally stop just to look around. The irony is that it's a sleepwalking induced and kindled by the notion that life is meant to be perpetual motion, as if life fully lived implies relentless activity.

"What are you doing?"

"Nothing."

"Nothing? How do you get away with that?"

Yesterday our birdfeeders were visited by three Cedar Waxwings. My wife and I sat watching through the glass doors that lead out onto our deck. Waxwings were a first for us. And they are surreal in their elegance. They are a crested bird, greyish brown with a canary yellow belly. Zorro-like, they wear a black mask and chin. Each looks like a fine porcelain figurine, delicate and without blemish. While we watched, a nuthatch shuttled from feeder to tree trunk, one sunflower seed per trip, each time wedging the seed into a crevice of the bark where he would, from my way of seeing, stand upside down while pecking away at the shell. The late spring evening sun hung as if suspended off the western horizon, while the air remained still.

Sometime during this pageant, it occurred to me that this is it. *This,* as in this elusive essence we call life. I tried to remember the Henry David Thoreau quote about going into the woods to drink from the very marrow of life, but I couldn't quite come up with it and realized that it didn't really matter anyway. I doubt that the Cedar Waxwings would have been impressed. If you are lucky, you grab hold of these moments when they come, for they are parcels of life undistilled. And you save the analysis for later on down the road. You could, I suppose, stop and take a picture if you wanted to take the time to find your camera. Or you can chuckle at your need to confine the moment, push it aside, and curl up on the couch to watch the birds, listen to their song, and feel the gooseflesh reminding you that your heart is still intact.

I love the story about Thoreau's visit to New York City. He reported, "I visited New York City last Tuesday, and met no real or living person."

There's also the wonderful movie, *Don Juan de Marco,* about a young man who believes he is Don Juan. A psychiatrist is given the job of curing him of his delusion, of bringing him back to reality. But the psychiatrist is intrigued by the boy's story and his infectious passion for life. The boy senses this. One day he says to the doctor, "You need me for a transfusion. It is only in my world that you can breathe."

There is no denying the fact that we live in a world where it is all too easy to opt for distraction, to create a life filled with obligations and meetings. It is something about an inherent need to justify our time as well spent. And to justify our passions and hobbies as valid. There is a consequence, to be sure. Frances Mayes recognizes this, writing of her time in Tuscany in her book *Bella Tuscany:* "Gradually, I fall into time [there]. At home in California, I operate against time. My agenda, stuffed with notes and business cards, is always with me, each day scribbled with appointments. Sometimes when I look at the week coming up, I know that I simply have to walk through it."

As time goes on—that time we operate against—we will feel a reluctance to let the magic happen. Something about holding back the cards that have been clutched so close to the chest, hedging our bets, not wanting all of our eggs in one basket, afraid to let go lest we be disappointed.

*Passion.* The very word puts some of us on edge.

*Enchantment.* Okay to describe a children's movie. But considered optional and no longer vital for the adult psyche.

The quirky movie with the sophisticated title, *Joe versus the Volcano,* is about a young man who has resigned himself to slogging through life. He puts in his time at a job he detests. He is hampered by persisting attacks from a "brain cloud," a supposedly fatal ailment. Through a bizarre twist, he's presented the chance to sail to an obscure island where he is to be offered as a sacrifice to the volcano gods. Believing that he will die anyway, he takes the offer. The trip, of course, awakens him from his soul-sick stupor. And for the first time, he notices. He sees. He feels gooseflesh. And he learns the lesson that it's not just where you look, but how.

This past winter, I looked outside my window, where the encasement of our Northwest winter had not yet released its grey stranglehold. Here in the Pacific Northwest, the perpetual winter grey can create a cavity that reduces your range of vision and stifles the spirit. The air was chilled and damp. I walked through the garden, on my way to other pressing projects, and felt immediately discouraged by the overall disarray, hardly expecting any signs of life to cheer me up. I was genuinely unnerved, greeted by the bright orange seed pods of the *Iris foetidissima,* the shy nodding blooms of the Christmas Rose Helebore, and the buds on our winter-blooming honeysuckle.

In my impatience—my hurry—I have often missed the beauty of the winter woodland. The trees are completely empty with the exception of a few stubborn alder leaves, yellowed and isolated as if notes of paper hung randomly to tell some traveler of the right path to take. That which had taken a backseat in the full bloom of spring and summer, now emerges: A stately cedar trunk, hidden through summer now stands erect and serene, surrounded by the mossy trunks of alder and the bent and glossy trunks of maple. At their feet congregate dozens of sword ferns—fronds glistening with the rain of late night—their polished forest green a sharp contrast to the brown and yellow and rust. The sun, not quite broken through the cloud cover, gives a subdued sense of backlighting with tones more sumptuous than I had noticed before.

Of course, you know what this means. We've come full circle. We're left with the undeniable correlation between enchantment and stillness. It is an odd mixture, to be sure. Stillness and enchantment. Waiting or slowing down enough to let the goose-flesh affect us, living the Sacrament of the Present Moment.

In our world, enchantment has been replaced by speed, acceleration, activity, and dizziness. Instead of enchantment, we are numbed and sedated, seduced by the glitter and hype, bombarded by the promise of bigger and better and more.

I heard a story from a friend about a couple who drove long and hard to the Grand Canyon. And of all things, they didn't stay but a few minutes. "It looked better on TV," they told my friend.

I had been ingrained to see life as a stage for achievement, requiring that I intentionally and willingly wear blinders. Living with such blinders always sets our sights beyond this day to what we will surely become or attain.

It is certainly no shame to be weaned on the milk of a dreamer. There is much good in ambition and aspiration, as long as it doesn't come at the expense of today's gifts and enchantments.

There is the old joke about the preacher and the priest and the rabbi talking about when life begins:

"When the egg and sperm touch," bellowed the preacher.

"When there is viability in the womb," cautioned the priest.

"No, no," said the rabbi, "Life begins when your kids leave home and your dog dies. That's when life begins."

It all started quite unintentionally, as do many such infatuations. I planted a few rows of vegetables, a few roses, and scattered two or three seed packets of annuals. And it all exacted something from me, arresting that part of my heart designed to engage life. It awakened something in me, that part of my childhood which fueled curiosity. I welcomed the alertness of that child, that ability to see again in vivid and exaggerated color. It mobilized something in me——a need to cherish and preserve, to protect and nurture.

A dreamer still. Oh yes. But I hope no longer isolated, no longer without a context, no longer relying only on the promises of tomorrow.

After tea is served alongside the reflector pool in my dreams, Earl Grey with Dorset cream melt-in-your-mouth shortbread, I drift back to the house. There I am curled up in a comfortable chair with another pot of steaming tea at my side. And I notice, with some pleasure, that the gooseflesh on my arms has not yet fully faded.

# SOUL GARDENING EXERCISES

## *Enchantment and Gooseflesh*

Find a comfortable chair where you can let your memory mean-der and recollect. Remember a place where you felt enchanted. Conjure the scene until you feel yourself squarely in the middle of it and feel the gooseflesh on your arms.

Where have your sacred places been? Where are the places of holy ground? What makes a place sacred or holy? If you have chil-dren, what do you teach them about sacred and holy places?

Design a dream garden. Or dream space. There are no good-taste-police to veto any of your choices. And there are no budget restrictions, so you might just as well go whole hog. If you feel comfortable, paint or draw your dream garden.

Spend an afternoon watching children at a zoo. Watch their wonderment, mesmerized by anything and everything unique.

Try a Navajo dawn walk. As you walk, be conscious that there is no distinction between what is scared and what is secular. Be aware that ordinary sights and sounds and smells and textures are infused with holiness.

*Quote for the day: "God does not die on the day we cease to believe in a personal deity. But we die on the day when our lives cease to be illu-mined by the steady radiance of wonder renewed daily, the source of which is beyond all reason" (Dag Hammarskjöld).*

# THE GRACE OF WONDER

*Dear Lord, grant me the grace of wonder.*
—Joshua Abraham Heschel

*In the morning I had been intoxicated by the spring air.*
*I had to do something*
*extravagant so I bought Mother a bunch of violets,*
*they smelled earthy and*
*wet and sweet, driving one crazy with longing for woods and peace.*
—May Sarton

I am back outside of Gloucester, England, visiting Camp Cottage and one of my gardening heroes, L. R. Holmes. It had been one year, but he recognizes me and seems genuinely glad I have returned to visit his garden. I walk around to see what is new.

Since my last visit, L. R.'s garden was highlighted on a popular British television series, *Victory Gardens.* His conversation on this day is stream of consciousness. "The BBC show was a real hit, and now I'm getting calls. That's the trouble with all this recognition, you certainly pay the price."

He has put in a new pond garden and has begun to clear another area near the back of the property for a bog garden. But one thing has not changed. L. R. is at home in this space, in this place, in sharing his garden with like-minded spirits. For all the hundreds who have traipsed through his garden over the past months, his enthusiasm has not waned. He still acts as a delighted tour guide for me, as if he is seeing his own garden for the very first time.

Gardening is about being present. In this life. Embracing the present moment can happen while we are observing, drinking in, and enjoying. For gardening is about seeing and serendipity, about celebration and connection, about the permission to waste time, and about the joy of sitting still. It can happen in times of planting, and watering, and harvesting. In times of resting, working, waiting, and dreaming. Times for letting the magic happen. Times for embracing the grace of wonder.

## Seeing

I was in a hurry, late to an urgent meeting that I now do not recall. So, I wanted to take a quick turn around the garden to see if there were any unnecessary messes needing later attention.

This was a few years back, when we had one of the mildest winters we'd had in some time. There was no hard freeze, so the bulbs and trees, duly tricked, began their spring pageant in mid-February. Some roses kept their foliage through the entire winter, the leaves on 'Graham Thomas' and 'Betty Prior' still a polished green.

The garden teetered between seasons, perennials gearing up for warmer weather. Several roses were off and running, tender laterals pushed out, rhubarb red and impervious to the reports that winter might not be finished. Many delphinium shoots, three or four inches tall, stood as miniature celery stalks, defying the slugs and the potential of a late winter frost. Rosettes of *Sedum* 'Autumn Joy' designed a vivid lime green against the peat-colored soil; small shoots of sweet woodruff seeped out between the cracks in the rockery; unassuming furry spindles of catmint, pushed up between the brittle twigs remaining from last summer, revealing our five cats' new summer playground; small mounds of foxglove appeared wherever the wind chose to deposit the seed; the nodding blooms of the Christmas rose Hellebore genuflected as shy residents standing among the dark green foliage; sturdy bright green blades of iris stood proud and upright, their spent stalks supine as a bridal train.

I walked around, utterly absorbed, charmed, and giddy in my delight, talking to myself, talking to the plants. I was in my own world—totally forgetting the urgent meeting—and wondered if anyone else lived this way. Our dogs, Conroy and Penny, lolled in the morning sun, ignoring their peculiar master.

There's a great Anthony de Mello story about the disciple who went to the master and said, "Could you give me a word of wisdom? Could you tell me something that would guide me through my days?" It was the master's day of silence, so he picked up a pad. It read, "Awareness." When the disciple saw it, he said, "This is too brief. Can you expand on it a bit?" So the master took back the pad and wrote, "Awareness, awareness, awareness." The disciple said, "Yes, but what does it mean?" The master took back the pad and wrote, "Awareness, awareness, awareness means—awareness."

## Serendipity

Serendipity is a week of clear winter days in Seattle. The air is crisp, the sun floats just above the tree tops as it moves diagonally across the southern sky, and the frost on the grass paths (from last night's temperature dip) glistens from the sun. Feeling energized, I attacked the still ominous pile of fireplace-destined, downed alder trees behind our house.

My wood cutting was interrupted by a visiting downy woodpecker, smallish with a sandalwood-colored underbelly and the characteristic black cap covering his head and back. Down the center of his back, a patch of sandalwood with small slashes of the same color along each side of the piece as if it had been sewn onto the bird's cape. Along the base of his neck he wore a brilliant ruby band.

His mood seemed carefree yet spirited as he hopped along the log not six feet from where I stood. As if programmed, he stopped after three or four hops, his head twitching much like the tics of a person with a severe caffeine addiction, where he enthusiastically probed and searched for breakfast.

I watched for some time, and he acted oblivious to my presence, at least, my presence as a threat. So he went about his business, living life the only way he knew how—non-self-consciously, heartily carrying out his morning mission.

I put down the chain saw. Wood cutting could wait. These are the times and places where we feel lucky.

On that, May Sarton and I certainly agree. She wrote in *Journal of Solitude:*

> This morning two small miracles took place. When, still in bed, I looked out of my window (it was a soft misty morning), it happened that 'light was on half the rock' out in the meadow. . . . I felt a stab of pure joy. Later . . . I stopped at the threshold of my study by a ray on a Korean chrysanthemum, lighting it up like a spotlight, deep red petals and Chinese yellow center, glowing. . . . Seeing it was like getting a transfusion of autumn light right to the vein.

## Celebration

There was a story in the *Seattle Times* about Buddy Ball, a youth sports program which mixes able-bodied children with children who have physical and developmental disabilities. The story honored Beth Campbell, creator of the program as a place for her developmentally disabled nine-year-old son, for her selection as National Volunteer Youth Coach of the Year:

> On Campbell's team, those who can't stand for long periods field from a stool. Those who can't find first base run with an

older buddy. It's typical for bases to be rounded in a motorized wheelchair. . . . To watch the wheelchair batter hit the ball deep and circle the bases with her hands raised and both teams cheering is a typical scene at Golden Eagle Buddy Ball games.

One parent talked about the time when Campbell decided that a boy with cerebral palsy would play outfield:

I saw Beth scoop him out of his bulky electric wheelchair, carry him to the outfield, and hold him on her knee so he could play outside the confines of his wheelchair. . . . He will probably never physically be able to catch a pop fly by himself . . . but now he knows what it feels like to be on the field and see a ball headed for him. You should have seen the look on his face. He grinned and laughed aloud as he worked to maintain his balance on her knee.

Campbell talked about her son:

He gets to first base and then runs into the crowd and hugs everybody. It's what sports should be: Kids running and jumping and playing. Nobody is keeping score. Nobody cares.

Celebration.

## Connection, Sense of Place

"This place," my wife tells me, "has always been medicine for my blue moods." In her book of essays titled *High Tide in Tucson,* Barbara Kingsolver writes of a similar sentiment:

This is the kind of April morning no other month can touch: the world is tinted in watercolor pastels of redbud, dogtooth violet, and gentle rain. The trees are beginning to shrug off winter; the dark leggy maple woods are shot through with gleaming constellations of white dogwood blossoms. I'm driving through deep forest near Cumberland Falls, Kentucky, winding across the Cumberland Plateau toward Horse Lick Creek. My daughter is quiet beside me in the front seat, until at last she sighs and says, with a child's poetic logic, "This reminds me of the place I always like to think about."

On an early afternoon last summer, I was sitting in my car on the ferry dock, passing the time reading a novel and counting seagulls. I couldn't help but overhear the conversation emanating from the car next to me, a conversation which turned out to be far more entertaining than the book I was attempting to read. There were two couples in the car, the younger I assumed to be the daughter and son-in-law of the older couple. This younger pair was vacationing from Southern California. They had all been visiting our island for the morning and were headed back to the parent's home on the Kitsap Peninsula. From the conversation, I gathered that they had planned to spend the entire day on our island.

"This is a pitiful island," the younger man decreed, parceling out each word slowly and distinctly, a novice stage actor spitting his enunciation.

I put my novel down. It could wait.

"I certainly didn't know what to expect," the father followed.

"Yeah," the younger woman began, her voice on the edge of pouting. "I expected a big beautiful shopping center. Like downtown Seattle. I thought the name Vashon Island rhymed with Fashion Island, so I expected something of the same."

Having lived in Southern California, I knew Fashion Island to be the name of a very upscale shopping enclave in Orange County.

"I was sure surprised," the mother chimed in, affirming her daughter with an apologetic tone that hinted she was sorry for wasting their day. "But I'm afraid you're right. There was absolutely nothing to see." She sounded taken aback.

"And the houses," the younger man again. "I didn't see any place I'd pay three hundred thousand dollars for. Did you?"

There were murmurs of assent.

As if to further clarify his insinuation, he added, "I sure couldn't live here."

"Well, you certainly wouldn't need to spend a whole day here," his wife elucidated. "I can't help but wonder what people who live here actually do. I mean, with their time."

She was on a roll. "I'm serious. I really did expect a nice shopping center. At the very least." Then her voice took on a sympathetic hue. "It must be quite a drag to go into Seattle anytime you want something."

"You mean, like, to have fun, or to get a life," the young husband added, followed by the affirming staccato laughter of his co-conspirators.

I wanted, of course, to lean out my window spewing some witty invective. But the best I could have mustered would have been a weak and blustery, "Damn it all, we have fun too!" After which, of course, I would have fallen silent, met by the stares of startled and blank faces, and not in any way knowing how to make our kind of fun sell. I simmered down.

I could have leaned out my window and told them about the view down through our canyon and the way the morning light can give a cedar bough translucence. Or the way the woodland smells each spring, of earth and cedar and decomposed leaves and the pungency of new life. Or the way a pileated woodpecker hammering on a tree trunk echoes through the canyon like remembrances of native drums. I could have pointed to the way the Olympic Mountains frame the view from the ferry deck or the way that the air fills your lungs with salted moisture and the vigor of life. I could have told them.

But I didn't.

Flannery O'Connor commented about a group of young upstart writers, "You know what's the matter with them? They're not from anywhere." Or, I can add, they've tried hard to erase those roots and the pull of the land, unaware of its power and importance.

Much of young adulthood is spent doing one's best to eradicate whatever scent is left over from the home country. Our fight for adulthood and individuation is often won at the cost of severing ties and burning bridges. Even so, Kingsolver writes of the hill country of Kentucky, "Forty years later it is still my 'home country,' it restores me still."

During my last trip to the house of my childhood, I walked the shore of Long Lake. Today, the wetland near my Michigan home is gone. And the shoreline of Long Lake is packed with cabins and cottages, the areas adjacent full of mobile homes and double-wides. Even so, I still wanted to climb that pine tree of my youth—still standing tall—to see what I could see. They are in your blood, these places, the boundaries that frame your notion of life and the world around you. But it takes awhile before they come into view.

## Permission to Waste

Yesterday was a Sunday. Lazy is always the adjective attached to such days, but it does not do justice. Is it a hint of the Puritan ethic, the guilt from wasting away the day, reinforced randomly and regularly to whomever may be near, with a yawn, "Sure is a lazy day."

Wasted? Perhaps. But what lavish, rich, and wonderful waste. We were terribly alive. For this Sunday afternoon did not bring with it the extraneous weight of an add-on or catch-up, or the hoped-for weightlessness of emptying or mindlessness. No, it was the full weight of life itself. At its richest. The full weight of the ordinary. The daily. The elements. Wasting a Sunday, not as a removal from life, but as an entry into life. Life felt fully without any diversions.

Suki, our cat, slept curled in a tight circle, locking my legs in a horizontal pose from couch to pine chest. I watched the rain through the panes of the family room window during the heavy lighting—the leaves a darker green, the tree shapes merging—of twilight. The room was warmed by a woodstove fire, begun eight hours before, as the day took shape. Strains of Bach, his Mass in C-minor, permeate the air, setting free "holy feelings." The pine chest coffee table strewn with bits of Sunday's paper, a "Calvin and Hobbes" comic clipped to be saved, magazines, books and a petal or two from the vase of tulips and camellias—a sign that a life was spent for this grace to be consumed.

The books lain askew are now new friends who took our hands—and our minds. Together, we soared to other times and places, to rivers and mountains and cities. We did so with laughter and tears and sadness and outrage. These friends then gently set us down in this warm and cozy family room, this rainy and lazy Sunday, ever more the richer. And glad to be alive.

Gardeners are an odd lot. We are isolated by our own peculiar tastes, from primroses to antique roses. From austere to gluttonous. From sedums to cedars. From cauliflower to sunflower. From jacaranda to 'Jackman's Blue.' From New York to California. From a single clay pot to acreage as far as the eye can see. We live in our own worlds, fueled by dreams and imagination and fancy. And yet, we are linked to gardeners past and present, sharing a common gusto for this experiment we call life. And this planet we call home.

People who love this world, people who pay attention, are gardeners. People who are invested, people who are aware. They are gardeners regardless of whether or not they have ever picked up a trowel. Because gardening is not just about digging. Or planting, for that matter. Gardening is about cherishing.

To cherish, one must be present. For this wonderful place we call home is not, as my upbringing insisted, some holding tank where we await transport to the gold streets up yonder. Susan Ertz has written that "millions long for immortality who do not know what to do with themselves on a rainy Sunday afternoon." She got that right. And it's clear to me now. If you can't find joy here, you will certainly be disappointed when you search for it in any life to come.

Another gardening season has come and gone here in western Washington. Islanders have busied themselves with the tasks of covering their dahlias, mulching their roses, and seeding their vegetable gardens with winter clover. Out of my study window I can see the bright rust-colored leaves of the purple Smoke Bush, doggedly hanging on until they're set loose by a serious cold spell. Nearby are the crabapple-sized rose hips clustered along the ends of the arching canes of *Rosa rugosa alba,* the nodding hazelnut-colored seed heads of bronze fennel, and the remaining lavender daisy blooms of *Chrysanthemum* 'Innocence,' slumped almost to the ground as if exhausted from holding their heads up for so long. It is mid-morning, and the sun sits behind the imposing madrone tree to the southeast of our house. Even so, rays filter through the leaves, and spiderwebs crisscrossing the garden glisten and dance in the streams of light. I sip my tea. And smile. Because I am enchanted here. And because I am a gardener.

And, it is good for my soul.

# SOUL GARDENING EXERCISES

## The Grace of Wonder

BLESSING PRAYER FOR A GARDEN
Lord of Creation,
who planted Your own garden called Eden,
come and bless this soil
which is to be our garden.
All that dies becomes earth,
And so it lives again.
May this garden soil
be both womb and tomb
a home for death and life,
so that seeds of living things,
of plants, of food and flowers,
may die and resurrect here in our garden.
Ancient earth,
our mystical mother,
teach us, your children,
that all things die
to nourish life.
Gentle earth,
be blessed with our love
as we work in you.
Make us mindful that one day
you will be our final bed
of love and ecstasy.
Amen.

WORKS REFERENCED

Bodo, Murray. *Walk in Beauty.* Cincinnati: St. Anthony Messenger Press, 1974.

Bonhoeffer, Dietrich. *Letters and Papers from Prison.* Indianapolis: Macmillan, 1981.

Bridges, William. *Transitions.* Reading, Mass.: Addison-Wesley, 1980.

Brookes, John. *The Country Garden.* New York: Crown Publishers Group, 1987.

Capon, Robert. *Between Noon and Three.* San Francisco: Harper & Row, 1982.

Cummings, Charles. *The Mystery of the Ordinary.* San Francisco: Harper & Row, 1982.

de Mello, Anthony. *Awareness.* New York: Doubleday, 1990.

————. *Song of the Bird.* New York: Image, 1982.

Dillard, Annie. *Pilgrim at Tinker Creek.* New York: Harper & Row, 1974.

Flaubert, Gustave. *Madame Bovary.* London: Penguin, 1950.

"Gardens that Grow People." *US News and World Report* 113, no. 9 (August 31, 1994): 24.

Hammarskjöld, Dag. *Markings.* New York: Knopf, 1965.

Hassel, David. *Dark Intimacy.* New York: Paulist Press, 1986.

Heschel, Joshua. *I Asked for Wonder.* New York: Crossroad, 1985.

Huizinga, Johan. *Homo Ludens.* Boston: Beacon, 1955.

Kelly, Thomas. *A Testament of Devotion*. New York: HarperCollins, 1992.

———. *Reality and the Spiritual World*. Philadelphia: Pendlehill Books, 1942.

Kennedy, Eugene. *The Trouble with Being Human*. New York: Image, 1986.

Kingsolver, Barbara. *High Tide in Tucson*. New York: Harper-Collins, 1995.

Lacey, Stephen. *The Startling Jungle*. Boston: Godine, 1990.

Lobel, Anthony. *Frog and Toad Together*. New York: Harper & Row, 1972.

Mayes, Frances. *Bella Tuscany*. New York: Broadway, 1999.

Merton, Thomas. *Raids on the Unspeakable*. New York: New Directions, 1964.

Mitchell, Henry. *On Gardening*. New York: Houghton Mifflin, 1968.

———. *One Man's Garden*. New York: Houghton Mifflin, 1992.

Neil, A. S. *Summerhill School*. New York: St. Martin's Press, 1995.

Osler, Mirabel. *Gentle Plea for Chaos*. New York: Simon & Schuster, 1989.

Pollan, Michael. *Second Nature*. New York: Dell, 1992.

Rybczynski, Witold. *Waiting for the Weekend*. New York: Penguin, 1991.

Sarton, May. *Among the Usual Days*. Edited by Susan Sherman. New York: Norton, 1993.

———. *Journal of Solitude*. New York: Norton, 1973.

————. *Plant Dreaming Deep.* New York: Norton, 1968.

Sheehy, Gail. *New Passages.* New York: Random House, 1995.

Vienne, Veronique. *The Art of Doing Nothing.* New York: Clarkson Pottery, 1998.

Vonnegut, Kurt. *Fates Worse than Death.* New York: Putnam, 1991.

Walker, Alice. *The Color Purple.* New York: Pocket Books, 1996.

Wilder, Louise Beebe. *Color in My Garden.* New York: Atlantic, 1990.

Williams, Sarah Lopez. "A Win-Win Attitude." *Seattle Times* (July 26, 1995).

Yalom, Irvin. *Love's Executioner.* New York: Basic Books, 1989.

Zen Roshi Story. Compare Hui-Neng Liu-Tsu-ta. *Platform Sutra of the 6th Patriarch: The Text of the Tun-Huang Manuscript.* Translated by Philip B. Yampolsky. New York: Columbia University Press, 1978.

*A Breath from Elsewhere* by Mirabel Osler. New York: Arcade, 1998.

*Clabbered Dirt, Sweet Grass* by Gary Paulsen. New York: Harcourt, Brace Jovanovich, 1992.

*Dakota* by Kathleen Norris. Boston: Houghton Mifflin, 1993.

*Gentle Plea for Chaos* by Mirabel Osler. New York: Simon & Schuster, 1989.

*Great Possessions* by David Kline. Seattle: North Point Press, 1992.

*Heart of the Land* by The Nature Conservancy. New York: Pantheon, 1994.

*Holy the Firm* by Annie Dillard. New York: Harper & Row, 1977.

*Journal of a Solitude* by May Sarton. New York: W. W. Norton, 1973.

*Second Nature* by Michael Pollan. New York: Dell, 1992.

*The Dream of the Earth* by Thomas Berry. San Francisco: Sierra Club Books, 1988.

*The Inviting Garden* by Allen Lacy. New York: Henry Holt, 1998.

*The Meadow* by James Galvin. New York: Henry Holt, 1992.

*The Solace of Open Spaces* by Gretel Ehrlich. New York: Penguin, 1985.

*The Song of the Bird* by Anthony de Mello. New York: Image, 1982.

*This Place on Earth* by Alan Durning. Seattle: Sasquatch, 1992.

*This Sacred Place* by W. Scott Olsen and Scott Cairns. University of Utah Press, 1996.

*Why We Garden* by Jim Nollman. New York: Henry Holt, 1994.

Made in the USA
Middletown, DE
03 September 2020